Oxford English for Careers

OIL AND G

C000257777

Lewis Lansford and D'Arcy Vallance

Student's Book

OXFORD
UNIVERSITY PRESS

Contents

1 An international industry

Kick off

Main oil producers

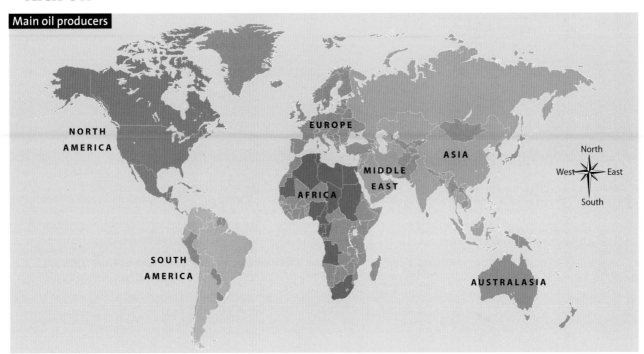

1 Study the map and discuss the questions.

1 Where is your country on the map?

2 Which regions are these countries in?

   a Algeria   e Malaysia
   b Brazil   f the UAE
   c Canada   g the UK
   d Kazakhstan   h the USA

3 Can you name ten more oil-producing countries?

4 Do you know the words to describe the nationalities for those countries?

   EXAMPLES
   an _Algerian_ worker
   a _Brazilian_ oil company

An oilfield

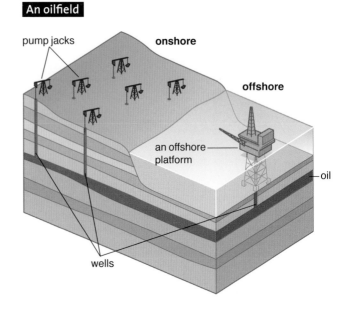

2 Read the sentences about the UK. Make sentences about your country.

1 There is a big oil and gas industry in the UK.
2 There are oilfields and gas fields.
3 There are many offshore wells.
4 They are in the north and the east.
5 There are not many onshore fields.
6 There is a big onshore field in the south.

In this unit
- the oil and gas industry: countries, locations, companies, employment
- *a / an / the*, the verb *be*
- spelling names and words aloud
- talking about numbers
- talking about tools and equipment

It's my job

1 🎧 Khaled Saleh is a technician in a big oil company. Where is he now? Listen and tick (✓) the correct boxes.

the USA ☐	the UAE ☐	plant ☐
inside ☐	outside ☐	control room ☐

2 🎧 Read the questions. Then listen again and answer them.

1 Why does he like his job?
2 Is he inside or outside today?
3 How many technicians are in his team?
4 How many men are outside with him?
5 Where are they from?
6 How do they speak to the control room?
7 What nationalities are there in the company?

3 Talk to Khaled. Make sentences like this:
Hello. My name's ...
I'm from ...
I like working inside / outside.
I like working in a big / small team.
I like / don't like speaking English.

Now tell your partner.

● Language spot

a / an / the
*Khaled is **a** technician in **an** oil company.*
*There's **a** man in **the** control room.*
*Khaled speaks to **the** man by radio.*
***the** UAE, India, **the** US, and Japan*

>> Go to **Grammar reference** p.118

Read the staff list and complete the sentences with *a, an, the,* or nothing.

> **Oxonoil**
> **Technical Department – staff list**
> Manager: John Smith (UK)
> Technicians: Lars Larsson (Norway)
> Greg Ford (US)
> Pierre Dupont (France)

1 Oxonoil is _____ small oil company.
2 John is _____ manager in the company.
3 John is _____ manager of _____ technical department. He is from _____ UK.
4 Pierre is _____ technician in _____ department. He is from _____ France.
5 Greg is _____ American technician.

Pronunciation

1 🎧 Listen and repeat.

1 A, H, J, K	4 I, Y	7 U, Q, W
2 B, C, D, E, G, P, T, V	5 O	
3 F, L, M, N, S, X, Z	6 R	

2 Say the letters in alphabetical order.

A B C D E F G H I J K L M N O P Q R S T U V W X Y Z

3 Work in pairs. Ask and answer.

1 How do you spell your first name?
2 How do you spell your family name?

4 Ask and answer about words on this page.

EXAMPLE
A *How do you spell team?*
B *T-E-A-M.*

Br E	Am E
zed	zee

Br E	Am E
store	store room / stock room

Number talk

1–199

1 Count 1–25 around the class.

2 Count in tens: 10, 20, 30, etc. to 90.

3 Study the information and say the numbers.

> **How to say numbers**
>
> **Telephone and reference numbers**
>
> 01238 = oh one two three eight
>
> (0 = *oh* or *zero*)
>
> **Quantities**
>
> 13 = thirteen   30 = thirty   33 = thirty-three
>
> 100 = a hundred (or one hundred)
>
> 101 = a hundred and one

4 Say these numbers.

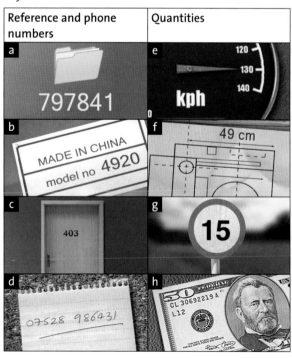

Reference and phone numbers	Quantities
a 797841	**e** 120 130 140 kph
b MADE IN CHINA model no 4920	**f** 49 cm
c 403	**g** 15
d 07528 986431	**h** 50 CL 30692219 A L12

5 Work in pairs. Student A, write four numbers between 100 and 199. Student B, say the numbers.

Change roles: B writes and A says the numbers.

6 Repeat **5** with four telephone numbers.

Listening

Conversations

1 🎧 Listen to four conversations. Number the pictures.

a

b

c

d

2 🎧 Listen again and complete the information.

1 The store is in building _____ in room _____ .

2 The technician needs _____ bolts.

3 The part number is _____ .

4 His employee number is _____ .

5 The store phone number is _____ .

3 Look at the listening script on p.125.

1 Do you understand it? If not, ask the teacher.

2 Work in pairs. Practise the four conversations.

3 Choose useful words or phrases to learn.

Useful phrases – getting repetition
Could you say that again, please?
Sorry?
What's that again?

Br E	Am E
spanner	wrench
wrench	adjustable wrench

Vocabulary

Tools and hardware

1 Which of these do you have at home?

a a screwdriver

e a wrench

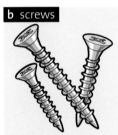

b screws

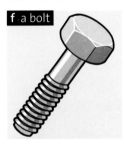

f a bolt

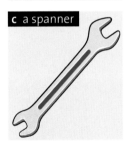

c a spanner

g an electric drill

d nuts

h washers

2 Practise this conversation.

  A *What's this in English?*
  B *It's a screwdriver.*
  A *What are these?*
  B *They're washers.*

3 Work in pairs. Point at the pictures, covering the labels, and have similar conversations.

Speaking

Checking

1 🎧 Look and listen. Then practise the conversation in pairs.

  A *What's in the box?*
  B *There are some bolts.*
  A *How many?*
  B *Twenty.*
  A *Good. What's the part number?*
  B *PD790.*
  A *What's that number again?*
  B *PD790.*
  A *The list says PD798. They're the wrong bolts.*

2 Work in pairs to find what's wrong (three things). Student A, go to p.106. Student B, look at these items and answer Student A's questions.

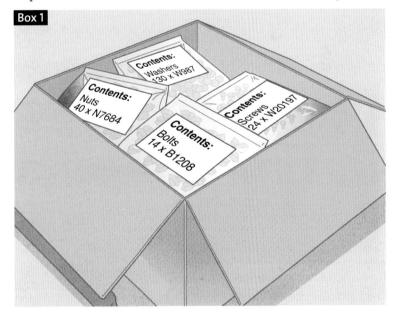

Box 1

Contents: Washers 130 x W987
Contents: Nuts 40 x N7684
Contents: Bolts 14 x B1208
Contents: Screws 24 x W20197

Now look at this list. Ask Student A *What's in box 2?* Find four things that are wrong.

Items	Part no.
120 bolts	B984
12 screws	R4197
140 nuts	N3521
140 washers	W3521

Reading

Employers

Read about the UK. Is your country similar or different? Write S (similar), D (different), or ? (I don't know) on the right.

Employers in the UK	Similar in my country?
Some countries have a national oil company (NOC), but there isn't an NOC in the UK. There are three other kinds of employer:	_____
1 Operating companies. These are IOCs (international oil companies) with famous names like Shell, Aramco, and ExxonMobil. They operate the wells and plants. There are smaller operating companies too.	_____
2 Drilling companies. The operating companies usually employ drilling companies for drilling wells. Some are foreign companies.	_____

Drilling for oil

3 Service companies supply equipment and technical services to the other companies. They also do special work, such as underwater work. There are a lot of service companies. _____

You can find a job with all these companies in newspapers, government job centres, and on the internet. _____

Project

Work in small groups. Find out about some oil and gas employers in your country.

Ask people. Look on the internet.

Write a few sentences about them. Use these cues.

1 Company name
2 Information about the company

> USEFUL WORDS
> *big / small*
> *IOC / NOC*
> *foreign / local*
> *operating company / service company*

3 Other information

• Language spot

The verb *be*

>> Go to **Grammar reference** p.118

1 Study the tables in the *Grammar reference* on p.118. Then complete the conversations.

1 Where _____ you from?
  I _____ from the UK.

2 What _____ her nationality?
  She _____ French.

3 _____ BP an American oil company?
  No, it _____ American. It's British.

4 _____ Gazprom and Rosneft British companies?
  No, they _____ . They _____ Russian.

5 Are you from the US?
  No, we _____ . We _____ from Canada.

2 Complete the questions about this book. Use *is there* and *are there*.

1 How many pages _____ in this book?
2 How many units _____ ?
3 _____ a word list at the back?
4 _____ a contents list at the front?
5 _____ six or eight pages per unit?

3 Ask and answer the questions above.

Writing

Completing a form

1 Read the information. Then write the dates in number form.

> **Writing dates**
>
> On forms, we usually write dates like this:
>
> *14/06/2010* or *14/06/10* or *14.06.2010* or *14.06.10*
>
> In American English, the month comes first: *06/14/2010*

1   4th February this year _____
2   17th November last year _____

2 🎧 You are starting a new job today: you are a fire officer in the Fire and Safety Department. Listen to your manager and complete the form.

> **Remember!**
>
> Names, titles, and nationalities begin with a capital letter.

International Oil Co.

First name _____

Family name _____

Employee no. _____

Manager _____

Department _____

Job title _____

Nationality _____

Date of birth (dd/mm/yyyy) _____

Telephone no. _____

Email _____

Signature _____

Date (dd/mm/yyyy) _____

Checklist

Assess your progress in this unit. Tick (✓) the statements which are true.

- [ ] I know words for countries, nationalities, numbers, and some hand tools
- [ ] I can talk about the oil industry in my country
- [ ] I can use *a* / *an* / *the* and the verb *be* correctly
- [ ] I can pronounce the letters of the alphabet and spell aloud
- [ ] I can check equipment
- [ ] I can complete a form with my information

Key words

Adjectives
foreign
international
offshore
onshore

Nouns
control room
drilling company
oilfield
oil well
operating company
plant
service company
team
technician

Verbs
operate
supply

Look back through this unit. Find five more words or expressions that you think are useful.

2 Upstream

Kick off

1 Read the information. Match the **bold** words with the explanations 1–6.

1 petrol / gasoline and diesel oil, for example
2 oil under the ground, usually dark brown
3 bring out or make
4 parts of an industry
5 the part that gets oil and gas out of the ground
6 the part that makes and sells useful products

2 Look at the pictures in this unit. Which pictures show

1 rocks?
2 a scientist?
3 hydrocarbons?
4 drilling a well?
5 a pipeline?
6 recording data?

Upstream and downstream

The oil and gas industry has two **sectors**: the **upstream** sector and the **downstream** sector.

Workers in the upstream sector find and **produce crude oil** and gas.

Workers in the downstream sector produce useful things from crude oil, like **fuel** for cars and planes.

Reading

The upstream process

1 Read the text on p. 11 and complete the four steps in this flow chart.

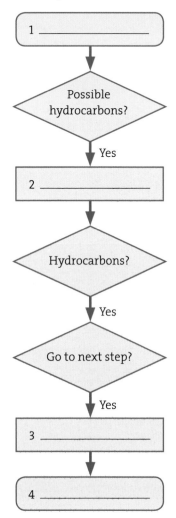

1 _____

↓

Possible hydrocarbons?

↓ Yes

2 _____

↓

Hydrocarbons?

↓ Yes

Go to next step?

↓ Yes

3 _____

↓

4 _____

2 Answer these questions about the text.

1 What do scientists try to find?
2 Do drillers always find hydrocarbons?
3 What do companies do before development?
4 Why do they build pipelines?
5 Which words mean

a difficulties? pr_____

b carry to another place? tr_____

c move continuously? f_____

3 Cover this page and look at the flow chart. Make two sentences about each of the four steps.

EXAMPLE

Step 1 is exploration. Scientists study ...

How do oil companies find oil and gas?

The first step is exploration. Scientists study rocks and do scientific tests. They look for rocks that can hold hydrocarbons.

What are hydrocarbons?

Oil and gas are made of hydrogen (H) and carbon (C). So we call them hydrocarbons.

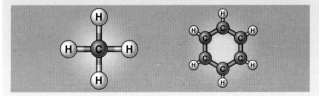

Do scientists find hydrocarbons?

No, they don't. They choose a good place for the next step: drilling. Drillers drill a well, and they sometimes find hydrocarbons.

Does production start immediately after drilling?

No. First the company does more tests and asks 'How much oil is there?' and 'Are there any problems?' If the results of the tests are good, they go to the next step: development.

What does *development* mean?

It means they prepare for production. For example, they build a pipeline to transport the oil.

How long does development take?

From a few weeks to many years. Then production starts. Crude oil and / or gas flow from the well and along the pipeline.

data (n) information, especially numbers

record (v) write data or enter data on a computer

skills (n) things that you can do well, for example, computer skills, languages, football

It's my job

1 Steve Dumontet tests wells before production starts. He answers questions like:

What is in with the oil? Water? Gas? Sand?

How fast does the oil flow up from the well?

Give your opinions. Does he need to

1 be fit?
2 be careful?
3 be good with numbers?
4 use a computer?

2 🎧 Study this information. Then listen and complete it.

Steve Dumontet

a **Company**	a Canadian oil company
b **Job**	a well test operator
c **Location**	different places in _____¹
d **A typical day**	prepare _____² equipment do _____³ and record _____⁴
e **Hours per day**	_____⁵
f **Start and finish**	_____⁶
g **Good things**	working _____⁷ seeing _____⁸
h **Skills**	_____⁹

3 Look at a–h in **2**. What was the question for each one?

EXAMPLE

a Company → *Who do you work for?*

4 🎧 Listen again and check your answers.

Vocabulary

Some upstream jobs

1 Match the jobs with the descriptions. Which jobs are in pictures in this unit?

Jobs

1 crane operator
2 driller
3 geologist
4 geotechnician
5 maintenance technician
6 pipe-fitter
7 production operator
8 roughneck

Descriptions

a studies rocks
b operates equipment to help geologists
c supervises a drilling crew
d works in a drilling crew under the driller's supervision
e operates a machine for lifting and moving heavy things
f fits pipes to make a pipeline
g services and repairs machines and equipment
h checks and operates production equipment

2 At which step or steps in the upstream process does each person usually work? Look again at the flow chart on p.10.

● Language spot

do and *does*, and *Wh-* questions

Do you work outside? Yes, I do.
Does he test rocks? No, he doesn't.
I don't like working long hours.
He doesn't work in an office.

1 Choose the correct words to complete the rules.

1 Use $\begin{array}{l} \text{do and } don't \\ \text{does and } doesn't \end{array}$ with *I, you, we, they.*

2 Use $\begin{array}{l} \text{do and } don't \\ \text{does and } doesn't \end{array}$ with *he, she, it.*

2 Choose the correct word to complete the questions.
1 *Do / Does* roughnecks work in offices?
2 *Do / Does* a driller supervise a drilling crew?
3 *Do / Does* a production operator fit pipes?
4 *Do / Does* a well test operator test rocks?
5 *Do / Does* geologists test wells?
6 *Do / Does* maintenance technicians repair things?

3 Ask and answer the questions in **2**.

EXAMPLE
A *Do roughnecks work in offices?*
B *No, they don't.*

4 Can you say these words correctly?
How   Where   When
Which   Who   Why

5 Which two letters do they all have?

6 Make questions and answers. (You need one or two words for each gap.)

1 **A** _____ Steve work?
  B He _____ in Canada.
2 **A** _____ he work for?
  B He _____ for a Canadian oil company.
3 **A** _____ many hours per day _____ you work?
  B I _____ eight hours a day.
4 **A** _____ you start in the morning?
  B I _____ at seven o'clock.
5 **A** _____ geologists do?
  B They _____ rocks and do scientific tests.
6 **A** _____ country _____ he work in?
  B He _____ in Russia.
7 **A** Why _____ they like the job?
  B _____ it because the money is good.
8 **A** How _____ oil companies find hydrocarbons?
  B _____ drill wells.

≫ Go to **Grammar reference** p.118

Speaking

Talking about jobs

1 Work in pairs. Student A, go to p.106. Student B, answer Student A's questions about Igor Kinsky. Then ask about Andrea Farrell and complete the information.

	Igor Kinsky	Andrea Farrell
Company	a Russian oil company	
Job	driller	
Where	Kazakhstan	
A typical day	supervise the drilling crew	
Hours per day	12	
Start and finish	7 a.m. to 7 p.m.	
Like	good money	

2 Student A, tell the class about Igor. Student B, tell the class about Andrea.

EXAMPLE
Igor Kinsky works for a …   *He works … hours*
He's a … in …   *He likes …*
On a typical day, …

Saying numbers

In American English, the *and* is sometimes left out:
two hundred nine (209). In British English, the *and*
is always used: two hundred and nine (209).

Number talk
Measuring oil and gas

1 Read the information and say the examples.

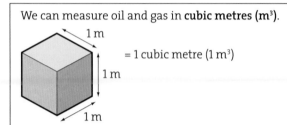

We can measure oil and gas in **cubic metres (m³)**.

1 m × 1 m × 1 m = 1 cubic metre (1 m³)

EXAMPLE
This field produces 100,000 cubic metres of gas per day (m³/d).
We use **litres (l)** for small quantities.
1 m³ = 1,000 l

EXAMPLE
Oil flows through the pipe at 10 litres per second (l/s).
US **barrels (bbl)** is another common measure.
1 barrel = 159 litres

EXAMPLE
This field produces 600,000 barrels of oil per day (bbl/d or bpd).

2 Say these quantities.
a 100 l   b 50 bbl   c 170 m³   d 12 l/s   e 28m³/hr

How to say large numbers

3 Read and say the numbers.

209 = two hundred and nine
380 = three hundred and eighty
3,000 = three thousand
4,444 = four thousand four hundred and forty-four
500,000 = five hundred thousand
560,000 = five hundred and sixty thousand
6,000,000 = six million
7,000,000,000 = seven billion

4 Say the numbers that the teacher writes.

5 Work in pairs. Student A, look at p.106. Dictate the numbers to Student B. Student B, listen and write the numbers.

6 Change roles. Student B, look at p.112.

Listening
Some big numbers

1 Look at the table and guess the approximate numbers.

Oil: the world uses ...	a _____ bbl/d b _____ l/d c _____ l/hr
Number of oil and gas fields in the world	d _____

The biggest field (Ghawar)
  location
  size
  oil production (bbl/d)
  oil production (m³/d)
  gas production (m³/d)
	e _____
	f _____
	g _____
	h _____
	i _____

2 Listen and complete the table in **1**.

3 Make a sentence about each item in the table.

Project

Find out about oil and / or gas fields in your country. Then write about them, answering the questions.

1 How many fields are there?
2 Which is the biggest field?
3 Where is it?
4 How big is it?
5 How much oil and / or gas does it produce per day?

Writing

Spelling: *e* – the most common letter

1 The letter *e* is the most common letter in English. Which of these words need an *e* at the end?

1 wher_____	5 operator_____
2 problem_____	6 company_____
3 writ_____	7 prepar_____
4 operat_____	8 pipelin_____

2 Which words need an *e* before the *s*?

1 produc_____s	5 supervis_____s
2 work_____s	6 ask_____s
3 start_____s	7 find_____s
4 studi_____s	8 lik_____s

3 Say where the *e* must go.

EXAMPLE
gologist: *between the first g and the o*

1 oil fild	5 drillr
2 companis	6 mony
3 machin	7 xploration
4 equipmnt	

4 Complete the words with *ee* or *ea*.

1 upstr_____m	5 n_____d
2 w_____ks	6 betw_____n
3 thr_____	7 h_____vy
4 sixt_____n	8 w_____ring

5 Work in pairs. Find words with *e* in this unit. Ask *How do you spell . . . ?*

Checklist

Assess your progress in this unit. Tick (✓) the statements which are true.

- [ ] I know key words for the upstream sector
- [ ] I can transfer information from a text to a flow chart
- [ ] I can use *do* and *does*
- [ ] I can use *Wh-* question words
- [ ] I can ask and answer about jobs in the upstream sector
- [ ] I can talk about oil and gas quantities and large numbers
- [ ] I can use the letter *e* correctly

Key words

Adjectives
downstream
upstream

Nouns
barrel
crane operator
cubic metre
development
driller
exploration
fuel
geologist
hydrocarbons
pipeline
production
rock
roughneck

Look back through this unit. Find five more words or expressions that you think are useful.

3 Downstream

Kick off

1 What do these people do in the upstream sector of the oil and gas industry?

driller   geologist   production operator   roughneck

2 Read and discuss the questions. Learn the **bold** words.

The downstream sector – what do you think?

Workers in the downstream sector make useful products from crude oil and natural gas. They **transport** these products and sell them.

1 Which of these things are made from oil or natural gas?

petrol
(Am E = gasoline)   **plastic bags**   **propane**   some **chemicals** in detergents   **asphalt**   some chemicals in fertilizers   tyres

2 Can you name ten more things containing oil products?

3 Crude oil goes from the well to a **refinery**. Refineries **separate** crude oil into **light** and **heavy** products, such as petrol (light) and asphalt (heavy).

These men work at an oil refinery. Are they opening a valve or checking data?

4 Gas and oil products get to us by sea, by road, by rail, and by pipeline. This driver transports petrol by road to **petrol stations** (Am E = filling stations).

In this picture, is he **loading** or **unloading** petrol?

5 Gas **processing plants** separate the different gases in natural gas.

Is this man measuring the pipe or looking for **leaks**?

● Language spot

Present Continuous

This man drives a petrol tanker.
Right now **he isn't driving**.
He's unloading *petrol.*

1 Answer these questions about the example above.

1 Does he drive a tanker?
2 Is he driving a tanker now?
3 What does he do?
4 What is he doing?

2 Choose the correct words to make the rule.

The Present Continuous uses *do / does* / *am / is / are* + *-ing*.

>> Go to **Grammar reference** p.119

3 Practise this telephone conversation.
A *Where are you now?*
B *I'm in the tanker.*
A *Are you driving?*
B *No. I'm having lunch.*

4 Have similar conversations with these phrases.

1 you now? / at the refinery
   working? / having a break
2 he now? / outside
   repairing something? / looking for leaks
3 they now? / at the plant
   collecting data? / testing pipes
4 she now? / in the manager's office
   talking to the manager? / waiting for him

5 We often use the Present Continuous for greetings and asking about progress, like the following examples.
1 *How are you doing?*
2 *How's it going?*
3 *How are you getting on?*

2 and 3 are usually about work or learning. 1 can be a general greeting. Some typical answers are
Fine, thanks.
OK, thanks.
OK, but I'm having trouble with …

Stand up! Greet three different people.

It's my job

1 Discuss these questions. Then read the text and check your answers.
1 What do petrochemical plants produce?
2 What happens in the control room?
3 How many hours per day do plants work?

Jang Li

I work at a big petrochemical plant. Petrochemical plants produce chemicals from hydrocarbons.
This plant gets light hydrocarbons from a refinery and produces ethylene (C_2H_4) and other important chemicals. Many industries use ethylene: for example, they use it to make plastics, detergents, and car tyres.

This plant produces two million tonnes of chemicals per year, and we control the production from this room. We use computers for this.

But computers can't do everything. We often need a technician to open or close a valve or check some data, so we use the telephone or radio too.

The plant works 24 hours a day, seven days a week, 365 days a year. So I often work at night. I work seven twelve-hour shifts every two weeks: that's four day shifts and three night shifts. This week I'm working night shifts.

2 Discuss these questions.
1 What does the plant produce, and why are the products important?
2 What skills does Jang Li need for her job?
3 How many hours does she work every two weeks?
4 Would you like her job? Why / why not?

Vocabulary

Computers and control panels

1 Match the words with a–k in the pictures.

button   hand-held computer   keypad   screen
control panel   key   knob   switch
gauge   keyboard   mouse

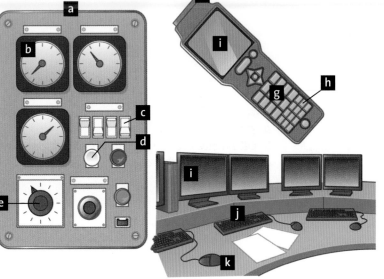

2 Work in pairs. Use the table below to ask and answer questions.

What's the thing What are the things	above below next to in on	the knob the screen	on the left? on the right?

EXAMPLE
A *What's the thing above the keyboard?*
B *That's a screen.*

3 You are having problems. Make sentences with the verbs in brackets.

EXAMPLE
The screen (not work) → *The screen isn't working.*

1 The screen (show) an error message.
2 The gauge (not work) properly.
3 The computer (make) a strange noise.
4 Some of the keys (not work).
5 The red light (flash).

Listening

Telephone calls and messages

1 What do you think people do in these departments in a company?

Technical Support
Human Resources (HR)

2 🎧 Listen to conversation 1. Write T (true) or F (false).

1 Omar wants to speak to Mike.
2 George is not working today.
3 There is a problem in the control room.

3 Mike is reporting the phone call. Is the information correct?

> That was the control room on the phone. They're having a technical problem. I'm going there now.

4 🎧 Listen again. Then report the call, but give more information.

5 🎧 Listen to conversation 2 and find the mistake in this written message.

Message

To: The shift supervisor

From: Faisal Hamdi

Of: (company/department): HR

Message:

Please call him about the new technicians, today if possible.

Caller's no.: 2223

Writing

Messages

1 Write messages for George in Technical Support, like the example. (Notice the changes: *I → he; him → you.*)

Mark

> Please tell George I want to talk to him about the new computers.

Message from: Mark

To: George

Message:

He wants to talk to you about the new computers

1 Mark

> Can George call me today?

2 Dan

> Please thank him for his message.

3 Bob

> I'm having trouble with my hand-held computer.

4 Jin

> We need some help with our new computers.

2 Write messages for Faisal Hamdi in Human Resources.

1

> Please send me file A407.

2

> Tell him I'm visiting the refinery today.

3

> Please tell him I can't meet him today.

Speaking

Making and taking calls

1 Choose the correct words.

A *Goodbye / Hello*[1]. Technical Support.

B Hi. Is *it / that*[2] George?

A No. *This / That*[3] is Ali speaking.

B Can I *speak / say*[4] to George, please?

A He's *talking / talks*[5] to the manager right now. Can I *take / get*[6] a message?

B Yes. *This / That*[7] is Andrew Watts *at / from*[8] Human Resources.

A Andrew Watts *at / from*[9] HR.

B Yes. I want to talk to George *about / on*[10] the new computers for our office.

B What's your *phone number / number phone*[11]?

A 3745.

B OK. *I'll give / I give*[12] him the message.

A *Thank / Thanks*[13] you.

2 Work in pairs. Practise the conversation.

3 Work in pairs. Student A, you work in Technical Support. Go to p.107. Student B, you work in Human Resources.

Conversation 1
Phone George in Technical Support. Thank him for repairing your computer. It is working well.

Conversation 2
Answer the phone. The caller wants Faisal Hamdi, but he is having lunch. Complete this message.

Message

To: _____

From: _____

Of: (company/department): _____

Message: _____

_____

_____

_____

Date: _____ **Time:** _____

Reading

News

1 Work in two groups, A and B. Read your group's news item. Find answers to these questions.

1 What is going up? Where?
2 Why?

A

Petrochemicals – a changing world

The top producers of petrochemicals are countries in North America and Europe. But this is changing. Now many countries in Asia and the Middle East are building new petrochemical plants, and petrochemical production is going up fast in these countries.

Saudi Arabia, for example, is hoping to be the number 3 producer in the petrochemical world in 2015.

This is good business because petrochemicals sell at higher prices than crude oil. It is good for employment too. Populations in Asia and the Middle East are going up, so these countries need new jobs for their young people.

B

Gas – going up

Oil and gas companies are planning to increase world gas production by 50% before 2030.

Big gas producers like Russia, Saudi Arabia, Qatar, Iran, and the UAE are increasing their production fast. Gas production in Africa, Europe, Asia, and the Americas is growing too.

Why are they doing this? Gas is becoming more important for many reasons. Petrochemical plants use a lot of gas, and the petrochemicals industry is growing. Oil is very expensive, so many other industries prefer gas too. CO_2 is bad for the environment, and gas produces less CO_2 than oil so many power stations around the world are changing their fuel from coal to gas.

2 Tell the other group about your news item.

3 Look at these sentences from the news items. Then complete the sentences below about yourself.

*Saudi Arabia, for example, **is hoping to** be the number 3 producer in the petrochemical world in 2015.*
*Oil and gas companies **are planning to** increase world gas production by 50% before 2030.*

1 I'm hoping to ...
2 I'm planning to ...

Pronunciation

1 🎧 Listen and underline the stressed part in these words.

Two-part words	Three-part words	Longer words
1 Europe	7 company	16 petrochemical
2 Qatar	8 industry	17 environment
3 business	9 Africa	18 refinery
4 because	10 example	
5 Iran	11 producer	
6 prefer	12 important	
	13 UAE	
	14 CO_2	
	15 Middle East	

2 Practise saying the words above correctly.

3 Can you say these words correctly?

Two parts	Three parts
1 countries	8 expensive
2 prices	9 Arabia
3 people	10 employment
4 before	11 increasing
5 produce	12 separate
6 reasons	13 chemicals
7 per cent (%)	14 ethylene

🎧 Listen and check.

4 Work in pairs. Take turns reading sentences from the news items aloud. Use the correct word stress.

Checklist

Assess your progress in this unit. Tick (✓) the statements which are true.

☐ I know key words for the downstream sector, computers, and control equipment

☐ I can use the Present Continuous

☐ I can describe problems with computers

☐ I can make and answer phone calls and take written messages

☐ I can understand the news items in this unit

☐ I can use word stress correctly

☐ I can talk about mathematical calculations

Number talk

Calculating

1 Match the words with the keys on the calculator.

1 plus / add
2 minus / subtract
3 times / multiplied by
4 over / divided by
5 equals
6 per cent
7 point
8 square root

2 🎧 We can do simple calculations in our heads. Listen and write the calculations.

EXAMPLE

A *What's seven point two five times three?*
B *That's twenty-one point seven five.*
You write: 7.25 × 3 = 21.75

1 _____   4 _____

2 _____   5 _____

3 _____

Check the calculations. Are they correct?

3 Look at the calculations in **2** and practise the conversations.

4 Say the calculations for these questions.

1 Li is working three twelve-hour night-shifts this week. How many hours is she working this week?
2 A petrol tanker has 18,500 litres of petrol in it now. It can carry 30,000 litres on the road. How much more petrol can the driver load into the tanker?
3 How many 8,000-litre tanks do you need for 32,000 litres of oil?
4 A refinery produces 6.2 million litres of petrol per day and 10.75 million litres of other products. What is the total daily production?

Key words

Adjectives
heavy
light

Nouns
chemical
department
Human Resources
petrochemical
processing plant
product
refinery
shift
Technical Support
valve

Verbs
load
separate
unload

Look back through this unit. Find five more words or expressions that you think are useful.

4 Safety first

Kick off

1 Point to these parts of your body. Say and learn:

ears   eyes   face   feet
fingers   hands   head

2 Look at the personal protection equipment (PPE). Complete the sentences below.

ear protectors

hard hat

face guard

boots

goggles

gloves

safety harness

respirator

1   A hard hat protects your _____ .
2   A face guard protects your _____ .
3   Boots protect your _____ .
4   _____ protect your ears from noise.
5   _____ protect your hands.
6   _____ protect your eyes.
7   A _____ protects you from smoke and dangerous fumes.
8   A _____ protects you from a fall.

3 Look at the pictures in this unit. What PPE are the people wearing?

Reading
Safety signs

1 Talk about the signs. Use these words.
COLOURS

black   blue   green   red   white   yellow

SHAPES

○ a circle   ▭ a rectangle   □ a square   △ a triangle

EXAMPLE
It's a blue and white circle.

2 Read the text about safety signs. Write these four headings in the correct places.
a   Green and white squares or rectangles
b   Black and yellow triangles
c   Red and white circles
d   Blue and white circles

Safety signs: colours and shapes

Safety signs are very important because the oil and gas industry has many hazards. (*Hazards* = possible dangers like electricity, chemicals, hot things, gas, machines, noise, falling objects, and slippery surfaces).

There are four main kinds of safety sign:

1 _____

These signs warn us about hazards. The signs give warnings like *Danger! Overhead crane* or *High voltage*.

2 _____

These signs usually have a red band across them. They tell us we must not do things. For example *Do not smoke here* or *Do not switch off this machine*.

3 _____

These signs tell us 'You must wear or do the thing in the picture'. For example *Wear goggles* or *Read the instructions before you use the machine*.

4 _____

These signs give information about safety. For example, they tell us *This way to the emergency exit* or *Lifejackets are here*.

3 What does each sign mean in **1**?

EXAMPLE
Sign number 1 means 'Wear goggles'.

4 Look at the list of hazards in paragraph 1. Say why they are hazardous.

EXAMPLE
Electricity can give you a dangerous shock.

USEFUL WORDS
noun
shock
verbs

| burn | cut | damage |
| hit | injure | poison |

Speaking
What does it mean?

1 Work in pairs. Practise this dialogue.
   A *What does the blue sign mean?*
   B *Which one?*
   A *The one with a man and a book. Can you see it?*
   B *Yes. That means 'Read the instructions before you use the machine.'*

2 Work in pairs. Have similar conversations. Student A, go to p.107. Don't show B. Student B, go to p.112. Don't show A.

3 When you have finished
   1 check your spelling
   2 underline and learn the new words.

attach (v) fit together

estimate (v) calculate approximately

prepare (v) make ready

1 tonne = 1 metric ton = 1,000 kg

1 ton (Am E) = 2,000 lbs

1 ton (Br E) = 2,240 lbs

It's my job

1 Study the information. Then

   1 say what is happening in the pictures.

   2 **estimate** the weight of the load in picture 2.

Riggers prepare lifting equipment. These riggers are erecting a rig to lift drilling pipes.

Riggers also work with crane operators. First, they attach slings to a load. Then the crane lifts the load.

2 🎧 Listen and answer.

   1 Which picture shows Danny?

   2 What is his opinion about safety?

3 🎧 Listen again. Then talk about Danny's job, using these words.

   1 high places   5 decide

   2 safety harness   6 in the sling

   3 lift ... move   7 every day

   4 weight ... size   8 hazards

4 Would you like Danny's job? Why / why not?

Number talk

Weights and measures

1 Write these abbreviations next to the correct words.

   cm   g   k   km   m   mm   t

   1 grams   _____   5 centimetres _____

   2 kilos   _____   6 metres   _____

   3 tonnes _____   7 kilometres _____

   4 millimetres _____

2 Can you pronounce these words correctly?

What's the ... ?	How ... is it?
length	long
width	wide
height	high
depth	deep
weight	heavy
speed	fast

🎧 Listen and check.

3 Say what we use these measures for.

EXAMPLE

(length)   *We measure the length of pipes and cables.*

4 Look at the pictures in *It's my job*. Estimate the length, width, and weight of the pipe, and the height of the rig.

EXAMPLE

A *How long is the pipe?*

B *About two metres, I guess. What do you think?*

A *Maybe 2.5 metres.*

5 Say what these signs mean.

EXAMPLE

1 *Maximum speed twenty kph.*

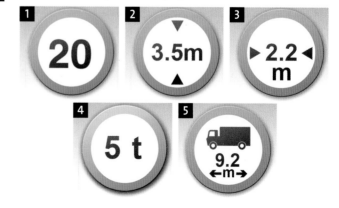

toolbox talk (n) a talk about safety
with tools and machines

Vocabulary
Which kind of word?

1 Read the sentences. Which **bold** words are

a nouns?   b verbs?   c adjectives?

1 He's a **good** crane **operator**.
2 He **operates** a **crane**.
3 He is **Canadian**. He **lives** in **Canada**.

2 Write the words in the correct places in the table.

calculate   driller   hazard   protect
safety   wide

Nouns	Verbs	Adjectives
width		1
2		safe
3		hazardous
protection	4	
calculator, calculation	5	
drill, 6	drill	

3 Choose the correct word.

1 This old machine isn't *safe / safety*.
2 He's an *Italy / Italian* engineer.
3 Can I use your *calculate / calculator*, please?
4 Refineries *produce / product* useful things from crude oil.
5 There are *hazards / hazardous* in my job.
6 How *depth / deep* is the well?
7 This company is a good *employ / employer*.

> **Learning words**
>
> When you learn a new word, always think *Which kind of word is it?*

4 What other questions can you ask about words?

1 ... mean?   4 ... spell it?
2 ... pronounce it? 5 ... stressed part?
3 ... a noun or a verb?

Look at the glossary at the back of this book. Which of these questions does it answer?

Listening
A toolbox talk

1 What is happening in the four pictures?

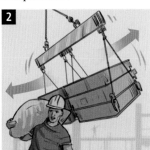

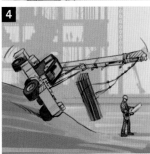

2 🎧 Listen to a supervisor talking to trainees about safety. Which hazards in **1** do they talk about?

3 🎧 Can you complete the rules? Listen again and check.

1 _____ under the load.
2 _____ to stop a swinging load.
3 _____ where you put your hands.
4 The hand signal for *Emergency stop* is

5 _____ always have radio contact with the crane operator.

4 How can you warn the men in pictures 1–4?
EXAMPLE
1 *Look out! The load's falling!*

● Language spot

Modal verb: *can*

1 Study this table and complete the conversation.

I He	can can't	lift 70 kilos.
Can	you he	lift 70 kilos?

A _____¹ *the crane lift 25 tonnes?*
B *No, it* _____². *It* _____³ *lift 20 tonnes,*
but it _____⁴ *lift 25 tonnes.*

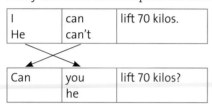

2 Work in pairs. Have similar conversations.
1 Can the tank hold 600 litres?
2 Can the bridge take a six-tonne truck?
3 Can the helicopter lift 7,000 kilos?
4 Can the crane do 30 kph?

3 Study situations 1 and 2. What can you say in situations 3–6?
1 asking permission

2 asking for help

3 You want to use your friend's phone. Ask him.
4 You are very hot. You want to take off your PPE. Ask the supervisor.
5 You must carry a heavy pipe. Ask someone to help you with it.
6 You don't know how to use the safety harness. Ask the supervisor to show you.

Modal verb: *must*

4 Explain these notices with *must* or *mustn't*.
EXAMPLE
You mustn't touch these switches.

>> Go to **Grammar reference** p.119

Writing

Spelling and notices

1 Add vowels (a, e, i, o, u) to make words.

1 pr___tect
2 faceg___ ___rd
3 s___rf___ce
4 d___ng___r
5 ___m___rg___ncy
6 c___rcl___
7 tr___ ___ngl___
8 r___ct___gl___
9 h___z___rd
10 t___ ___ch

2 Your boss wants you to write short safety notices (3–5 words maximum). Read his instructions.

1 Where should you put each notice?
2 Write big notices like the notices on p.26.

1 'This surface is slippery. We don't have a sign, so we must write a notice. Can you write it, please?'

2 'This machine isn't safe, so people mustn't use it. Put a notice there, please.'

3 'Some boxes are blocking the fire exit. We mustn't block fire exits. Move the boxes and put a notice up.'

4 'Some visitors don't wear hard hats. They think that visitors don't need hard hats. But they must wear them.'

Key words

Adjective
slippery

Nouns
crane
emergency
fumes
hazard
rigger
rule
safety
shock
sign
signal

Verbs
damage
injure
protect
warn

Look back through this unit. Find five more words or expressions that you think are useful.

5 Finding oil and gas

Kick off

1 Look at the diagrams in this unit. Which diagrams are

    1 about geology?   4 two-dimensional (2D)?
    2 about physics?   5 three-dimensional (3D)?
    3 about technology?

2 Look at this picture. Give your opinions.

    1 What is on the screen?
    2 What do the colours mean?
    3 What kind of glasses are the people wearing?
    4 Who are the people?
    5 What are they looking for?

Vocabulary

Some science

1 What do these people study and know about?
a geologist   a physicist   a geophysicist

2 Study diagram 1 and discuss the questions.

    1 Which rock can hold water, oil, and gas?
    2 Which rock is hard and very solid?
    3 Why is the gas above the oil?
    4 Why can't the gas go up to the surface?

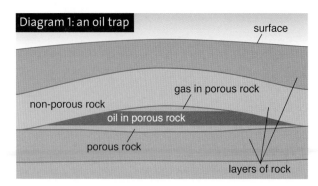

Diagram 1: an oil trap

3 Study diagram 2 and complete the sentences.

    1 Vibrations produce _____ .
    2 A microphone converts sound waves into
       _____ .

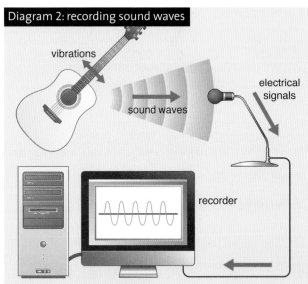

Diagram 2: recording sound waves

4 Look at diagram 3. Then give an example of

    1 a reflector that reflects light waves
    2 other kinds of wave
    3 waves that travel fast
    4 waves that travel slowly.

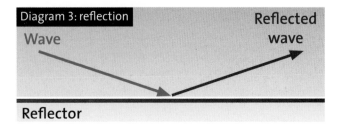

Diagram 3: reflection

In this unit
- key vocabulary for the science of exploration
- pronunciation: sentence stress
- sentence structure and word order
- listening to instructions
- describing specifications

Reading

Seismic exploration

1 Where do you find an oil trap? What is in it and why?

2 Study this diagram. What do you think the trucks and the geophones do?

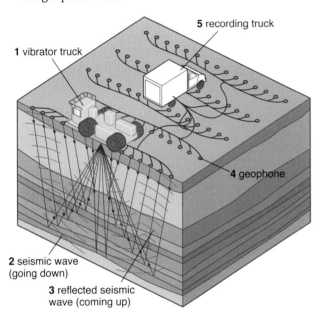

1 vibrator truck
5 recording truck
4 geophone
2 seismic wave (going down)
3 reflected seismic wave (coming up)

3 Read the text. Write T (true) or F (false).

1 Oil companies make maps of the surface.
2 Seismic waves can't go through rocks.
3 Vibrator trucks make seismic waves.
4 One rock layer reflects all the waves.
5 Geophones send electrical signals to the recording truck.
6 The geophones produce 3D maps.

4 The word *they* is in the text nine times. It can mean different things in different sentences. Find every *they* and say what it means.

EXAMPLE

In paragraph 1, they *means oil companies.*

5 Look at the labels (1–5) in the diagram above and explain the process. Begin: *Vibrator trucks make seismic waves. The waves go . . .*

6 Look at the diagram of seismic reflection at sea and explain that process.

How to find oil traps

Drilling is expensive. So oil companies plan carefully before they start drilling. First they make 3D maps of the rocks below the surface. Then they study these maps carefully. They look for possible oil traps.

How do they make these maps? How do they find out what is below the surface? The answer is 'seismic waves'.

Seismic waves are sound waves, and they can travel through rock layers.

Most oil companies use vibrator trucks to make seismic waves. These heavy trucks make vibrations on the surface, and the vibrations send waves down to the rocks below.

Each rock layer reflects some of the waves. The reflected waves travel up to geophones on the surface. Geophones are like microphones: they convert the waves into electrical signals. A machine in the recording truck records the signals. Computers can convert these signals into 3D maps.

Seismic reflection works at sea too. But the crews use hydrophones, not geophones, and they use an underwater gun to make seismic waves.

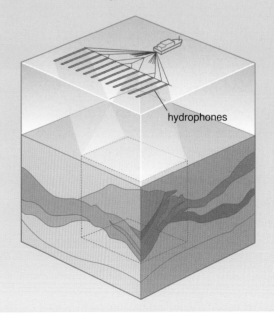

hydrophones

GPS (Global Positioning System) A GPS unit tells you your exact position on Earth. It can also show you the way to other positions.

sat nav (satellite navigation) A sat nav unit uses GPS to show the way on a map. Many cars have these units.

It's my job

1 Faisal Abdel Latif is a geotechnician. He works in a seismic survey crew. Look at the picture and answer the questions.

1 What is Faisal carrying on his back?
2 What electronic gadget is he holding?
3 What is he using it for?

🎧 Listen and check your answers.

2 🎧 Read these questions. Then listen again.

1 What does Faisal do?
2 What must he do carefully?
3 How do the different crews communicate?
4 Why must Faisal be fit?

3 🎧 Listen again to the last part and complete the notes.

Things he likes

1 being _____ and seeing different _____
2 working in a _____
3 the _____

4 Would you like Faisal's job? Why / why not?

Pronunciation

1 🎧 Listen to these sentences. Underline the stressed words as in the example.

EXAMPLE

We <u>must</u> put the <u>geophones</u> in the <u>right place</u>.

1 That's very important.
2 So we all have a GPS unit.
3 The GPS tells you your exact position.
4 We read the data carefully to get the position right.

2 Practise saying the sentences above.

3 In English, we stress the most important words (important = important for understanding). Is this the same in your language?

4 Which words would you stress in these sentences? Underline them.

1 This job can be hard work.
2 You're walking a lot and carrying heavy things.
3 So you must be fit.
4 I like the job.
5 I like it for two reasons.
6 I love being outside and seeing different places.
7 And I like working in a team.
8 And the money's good too.
9 That's three reasons, isn't it?!

5 🎧 Listen to the sentences in **4**. Did you underline the same words? Discuss any differences.

● Language spot

Words in sentences

noun	verb	noun	adverb
1 *Faisal*	*places*	*the geophones*	*carefully.*

2 *He works in hot weather and difficult places.*

| pronoun | | adjectives | noun |

Faisal and *He* = the SUBJECT

geophones = the OBJECT in sentence 1

There are three kinds of sentence:

Questions (e.g. *Who is he?*)

Statements (e.g. *He is Faisal.*)

Imperatives (e.g. *Stop!*)

1 What kind of word is each underlined word? What kind of sentence is it?

EXAMPLE

Don't <u>forget</u> your GPS.

Forget is a verb. The sentence is an imperative.

1 <u>Faisal</u> <u>usually</u> does the work <u>quickly</u>.
2 <u>He</u> likes <u>it</u>, and the money is <u>good</u>.
3 It's very hot in the <u>desert</u> in <u>summer</u>.
4 <u>Is</u> my <u>new</u> <u>radio</u> in the truck?

2 Find examples of these rules in **1**. Is the rule different in your language or the same?

1 The subject is before the verb in statements.
2 Adjectives are usually before nouns or after *be*.
3 Adverbs are never between a verb and an object.
4 The subject can be a noun or a pronoun, but we don't write both. (*Faisal he likes his job.*)
5 Phrases about times and places usually go at the end of a sentence.
6 Imperatives don't usually have a subject.

3 Look at the words in brackets. Where must we put them to make correct sentences?

1 (porous) We find oil and gas in rocks.
2 (reflect) Mirrors light waves very well.
3 (badly) Black things reflect light waves.
4 (every day) He works outside.
5 (exact) What's your position?

4 In the sentences below, change the underlined words to the correct pronoun.

	Subject pronouns	Object pronouns
Singular	*I, you, he, she, it*	*me, you, him, her, it*
Plural	*we, you, they*	*us, you, them*

EXAMPLE

<u>Mr Jones</u> wants to talk to <u>you and me</u>. →

He wants to talk to us.

1 <u>Faisal</u> is helping <u>Ali and Hamid</u>.
2 <u>The drivers</u> can talk to <u>the man</u> by radio.
3 <u>My friends and I</u> don't like hot weather.
4 <u>Mr Ali</u> has a message for <u>me and all the technicians</u>.
5 <u>The woman in HR</u> has the forms.

5 Put these words in the correct order to make sentences.

1 the / him / is / talking to / geologist
2 read / carefully / the / data / seismic
3 can / me / help / you ?
4 have / I / at the refinery / a job
5 job / a / good / and / it / it's / I / like

>> Go to **Grammar reference** p.120

Writing

Writing sentences

There are eight sentences in the paragraph below. Separate the sentences and write the paragraph correctly.

sentences always begin with a capital letter statements always have a full stop at the end questions have a question mark imperatives have a full stop or sometimes an exclamation mark why is this important it is important because it helps us to understand sentences some nouns always have capital letters too the names of people and places are two examples

Br E	Am E
full stop	period

Number talk

Global positioning

1 Match the words in the list with a–e in the diagram.

latitude   longitude   receiver
satellite   signal

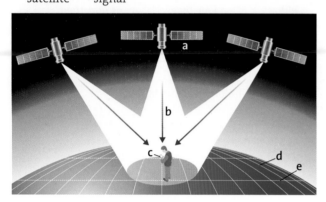

2 Look at the screen of this GPS receiver. What do the following mean? Say them correctly.

N   S   E   W   322°   LAT   LON   54.9220°

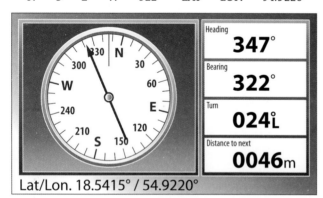

Heading	**347°**
Bearing	**322°**
Turn	**024°L**
Distance to next	**0046m**

Lat/Lon. 18.5415° / 54.9220°

3 Find these words in the glossary at the back of this book. Then complete the radio conversation.

bearing   coordinates   heading   position
waypoint

You	What's your _____ [1] now?
Faisal	My _____ [2] are 18.5415 degrees by 54.9220 degrees.
You	How far is the next _____ [3]?
Faisal	Just 46 metres.
You	What's your _____ [4]?
Faisal	347 degrees. But the correct _____ [5] is 322, so I must go left 24 degrees.

Listening

How to use GPS

1 🎧 A trainee is learning how to use GPS. Read the notes, then listen to the trainer and complete the notes.

GPS – Global Positioning System

Uses

to find your exact position on the Earth

to navigate to other positions (waypoints)

HOW TO NAVIGATE

Before the trip,

Enter and save the coordinates of all _____ a

At the start of the trip,

1 Turn on the GPS.

2 Wait until it receives signals from _____ b
  satellites.

3 It shows the _____ c of your position.

4 Select the first _____ d.

5 Select GOTO.

6 Follow _____ e.

2 Work in pairs. Student A, cover the trainee's notes. Tell B how to use GPS, using the notes below. Student B, listen and help if necessary. Then change roles.

NOTES
1 Before your trip, ...
2 At the start of the trip, ...
3 Wait until ...
4 Then it shows ...
5 Select ...
6 Select ...
7 Follow ...

Speaking

Discussing specs

1 Read the specs (specifications) and make a question about each one.

EXAMPLES
How many channels does it have?
What are the dimensions?

The T60 two-way radio

channels: 6

dimensions: 54 × 140 × 25 mm

weight: 190 g

colour: black

material: plastic

maximum range: 18 km

battery life: 36 hours

water resistant: no

shock resistant: yes

sand and dust resistant: yes

separate clip-on microphone: no

display screen: no

controls: channel selector knob, volume control, on/off switch, press-to-talk button

USEFUL LANGUAGE: DIMENSIONS
1 m × 2 m × 4 m
= *One metre **by** two metres **by** four metres.*

2 Work in pairs. Student A, go to p.107. Student B, go to p.112.

3 Work in pairs. Read about Sandro and choose the best radio for him. Then explain your choice to the class.

> Sandro is a geotechnician in Brazil. He often works outside. He sometimes works in bad weather and heavy rain. He often carries heavy equipment. He needs to talk by radio to other people in his team. He often needs to use his hands for other things while he talks. He is sometimes away from base for 36 hours.

Checklist

Assess your progress in this unit. Tick (✓) the statements which are true.

- [ ] I know some key words in geology, physics, and exploration technology
- [ ] I can use sentence stress
- [ ] I know some rules about sentence structure and I can use correct word order
- [ ] I can talk about GPS, positioning, and navigation
- [ ] I can understand some spoken instructions
- [ ] I can discuss some specifications

Key words

Adjective
seismic

Nouns
bearing
coordinates
geophone
heading
layer
position
signal
truck
vibration
wave
waypoint

Verbs
convert
record
reflect

Look back through this unit. Find five more words or expressions that you think are useful.

6 Drilling

Kick off

1 Study these simplified diagrams and the words. Then discuss the questions below.

1 Which part rotates and drills through rock?
2 What is between the bit and the surface?
3 Where do the pipes stand before they go into the hole?
4 What tall thing supports the lifting equipment and the drill string?
5 What does the rotary table do to the drill string?
6 What is mud?
7 Which machine sends mud down to the bit?
8 What comes up to the surface with the mud?
9 For deep wells, the derrick must be very strong. Why?

2 Complete the description of the mud process. Use words from the diagrams.

Drilling mud is a mixture of water, clay, and other materials. The _____¹ pumps mud from the _____² into the top of the drill string. The mud flows down inside the _____³ to the bit. It cleans and cools the _____⁴. Then it flows up the hole and carries _____⁵ up with it. The mud and cuttings go to the _____⁶. The mud screen separates the cuttings from the mud. The mud flows through to the _____⁷ below.

3 🎧 Listen and check your answers above.

4 Can you guess: how deep is the deepest well in the world? Find out later in this unit.

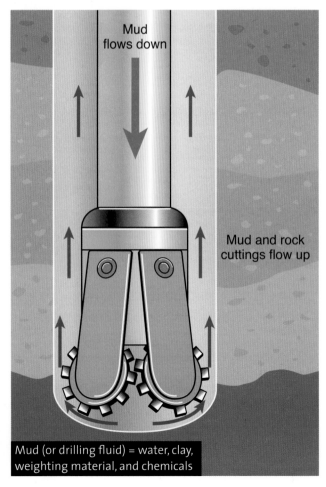

Mud (or drilling fluid) = water, clay, weighting material, and chemicals

Labels on left diagram: derrick, drill pipes, lifting equipment, monkey board, motor, flow of mud, mud pump, pipe rack, mud screen, mud tank, flow of mud, rotary table, drill string (drill pipes), drill bit

Labels on right diagram: Mud flows down, Mud and rock cuttings flow up

In this unit
- key vocabulary for drilling work
- problems, solutions, instructions
- adjective forms
- pronunciation and spelling
- giving safety advice

Reading

A drilling crew

1 Read the text. Then answer the questions.
Which person / people

1 are usually the youngest and most junior?
2 is usually the oldest and most senior?
3 need to be strong? Why?
4 is not afraid of high places?
5 must watch gauges or screens carefully? Why?
6 needs a desk and a telephone? Why?

2 Use information in the text to talk about the pictures
on this page and on p.10.

3 Choose the correct words. Explain your choices.
1 Roustabouts do _____ work.
   a skilled   b hard   c desk
2 Roughnecks usually prepare the _____ .
   a drill string   b mud   c hole
3 Derrickmen should wear _____ .
   a face guards   b glasses   c a safety harness
4 The driller helps the crew to _____ .
   a learn   b clean equipment   c lift things
5 The rig manager _____ new equipment.
   a makes   b repairs   c orders

Who are the people in a typical drilling crew?

Roustabouts are often the youngest people in a drilling crew. They clean, maintain, and move equipment and help the other workers. Roustabouts want better jobs, so they work hard, listen carefully, and learn fast.

Roughnecks are like roustabouts, but they are more skilled. They work on the drilling floor. They connect the heavy drill pipes and put them into the hole, or they disconnect the pipes as they come up out of the hole.

The **derrickman** works high up on the monkey board about 25 metres above the floor. He guides the top part of the drill pipe. At other times, he helps the mud engineer (or 'mud man'): he checks the mud and maintains the pump. The mud must not be too thick or too thin, and the pump must keep working.

The **driller** supervises and trains the drilling crew, and he controls the drilling equipment. For example, he operates the motor that lifts the drill pipes. He controls the speed of the drill, which must not be too fast or too slow. On very modern rigs, the driller sits in a special driller's chair. The chair has joystick controls and display screens – like a computer game.

The **rig manager** or **toolpusher** is the most senior person in the drilling crew. He is usually the oldest and most experienced person too. He makes sure the crew has all the right equipment. He is responsible for their safety and for paperwork.

The **mud pump** is one of the largest and heaviest parts of a drilling rig, and one of the most difficult parts to transport.

Listening

Problems and solutions

1 Can you give some examples of thin fluids and thick fluids?

EXAMPLES

Thin	Thick
water	*honey*

2 What is drilling mud and what does it do? Use the words in the list.

Nouns

bit   clay   cuttings   mixture   water

Verbs

bring   clean   cool   lubricate

3 🎧 Listen to these conversations at a drilling rig and complete the problems.

Problem 1	_____[1] aren't coming up to the surface
Why?	The mud is too thin
Solution	Make it thicker
How?	Add _____[2] kilos of clay

Problem 2	The _____[3] is very noisy
Why?	The mud is too _____[4]
Solution	Make it thinner
How?	Add _____[5] litres of water

Problem 3	The drilling floor isn't _____[6]
Why?	There's a lot of _____[7]
Solution	_____[8] the floor
How?	With _____[9]

4 🎧 Listen again and complete all the information.

5 🎧 Look at the listening script on p.127. Choose one conversation and listen for the pronunciation. Notice the stressed words and the sounds.

6 Work in pairs. Practise the conversation.

● Language spot

Adjective forms

1 Match the opposites.

1	thick	a	narrow
2	long	b	light
3	heavy	c	thin
4	wide	d	low
5	noisy	e	short
6	big	f	cold
7	deep	g	small
8	high	h	weak
9	strong	i	shallow
10	hot	j	quiet
11	difficult	k	approximate
12	important	l	safe
13	dangerous	m	easy
14	exact	n	unimportant

2 Read the examples and answer the questions.

   a *The mud is **too thin**.*
   b *The mud isn't **thick enough**.*
   c *Make it **thicker**.*
   d *Make it **more viscous**.*

   1 Which sentences have the same meaning?
   2 Why do we say *thick + er* but *more + viscous*?

>> Go to **Grammar reference** p.120

3 Complete the conversations about problems.

   1 Problem: a small wrench
      A The wrench isn't _____ .
      B We need a _____ one.
   2 Problem: a short bolt
      A The bolt is _____ .
      B I'll get a _____ one.
   3 Problem: a dangerous job
      A This job is _____ .
      B Yes. I want a _____ job.
   4 Problem: cold water
      A The water isn't _____ .
      B It should be _____ .
   5 Problem: a narrow walkway
      A The walkway is _____ .
      B We must make it _____ .

Br E	Am E
maths	math

4 Complete the questions, changing the word in brackets to *more* + adjective or adjective + *-er*.

1 Which is (difficult): maths or English?
2 Which is (long): a kilometre or a mile?
3 Which is (important): speed or safety?
4 Which is (cold): Canada or the USA?
5 Which is (dangerous): fire or H_2S gas?
6 Which is (big): Russia or China?

Now discuss the questions.

5 Read the examples and answer the questions below.

The comparative form (*-er* / *more*):
*Who is **older**: Jack or Hamid?*
*And who is **more experienced**?*

The superlative form (*-est* / *most*)
Who is **the oldest** person here?
Who is **the most senior** person in the crew?

1 Which form compares only two things?
2 Which form means 'Number 1' of many things?

6 Complete the sentences. Use the superlative form of the adjectives in the list.

big   deep   dirty   experienced
junior   old

1 Roustabouts are the _____ people on an oil rig and they do the _____ jobs.
2 The toolpusher is usually the _____ and the _____ person on a rig.
3 The _____ well in the world is 10,685 metres. The well is in the Gulf of Mexico and belongs to BP, one of the _____ International Oil Companies.

Pronunciation

1 🎧 Listen to these words. Can you hear the /r/ sound? Underline the r if you can hear it. If the r is silent, cross it out.

1 roughneck
2 dirty
3 senior
4 older
5 crew
6 operate
7 control
8 heavier

2 Look at these words and tick (✓) the correct boxes.

letter r + sound	examples	/r/	/r/
r + vowel sound	*drill, strong*	✓	–
r + consonant sound	*hard, works*		
r + nothing	*bigger, older*		

3 Which of these words have a silent r?

1 longer
2 problem
3 important
4 drill
5 shorter
6 worker
7 strong
8 deeper

Now say the words. Practise in pairs.

Writing

Spelling: single and double letters

1 Complete these words with one or two letters. Use the letter in brackets.

1 (l) dri*ll*   oi*l*   sha____ow
2 (g) bi____   bi____er   bi____est
3 (n) begi____   begi____ing   thi____er
4 (p) sto____   sto____ing   dee____er
5 (r) a____ive   cont____ol   co____ect
6 (s) gla____es   ea____y   vi____cous
7 (t) ho____   ho____er   ho____est

2 Find more words with double letters in this unit.

ff	difficult
tt	cuttings

Speaking

Giving safety advice

1 The pictures are from a safety manual for drilling crews. Which person is

1 wearing loose clothes?
2 standing under a load?
3 running up or down steps?
4 eating near chemicals?
5 handling chemicals without PPE?
6 walking below people working?
7 standing between a wall and a moving load?
8 using a broken tool?
9 climbing without a safety harness?
10 doing the right thing: lifting correctly and keeping his back straight?

2 Say what might happen in each situation.

EXAMPLE
Machines might catch his loose clothes and injure him.

3 Work in pairs. You work in a drilling crew. You are looking after a new person in the crew. Take turns advising him.

EXAMPLE
You shouldn't wear loose clothes because machines might catch them.

Vocabulary

Understanding instructions

1 Underline the verbs that tell you what to do.

EXAMPLE
I want you to <u>load</u> the truck.

1 Clean the floor.
2 Climb up to the monkey board.
3 You need to tighten that loose bolt.
4 I want you to dig a hole.
5 Those boxes shouldn't be on the floor. Move them now.
6 Unload those pipes from the truck.
7 See those pipes? Stack them on the rack.
8 Guide the pipe into position.
9 Today, you're painting the tank.
10 Connect the new hose to the pump.
11 Pour this chemical into the pipe.
12 The bit might be damaged. Inspect it carefully.

2 Explain or mime the meaning of each underlined verb.

3 Work in pairs. Student A, say instructions. Student B, say 'OK' and mime the action.

Project

1 Read the questionnaire. Discuss the reasons for each question.

2 Which are the three most important questions? Give your opinion.

3 Work in pairs. Ask and answer the questions. (3 = Yes; 2 = Maybe; 1 = No) Then add up your score. Is drilling the job for you and your partner?

Key words

Adjectives
thick (= viscous)
thin

Nouns
derrick
derrickman
drill bit
drill string
motor
mud
pump
roustabout
toolpusher

Verbs
connect
disconnect
guide
tighten

Look back through this unit. Find five more words or expressions that you think are useful.

7 Pipes and pipelines

Kick off

1 Match the names with 1–8 in the picture.

a flanged joint
b tee
c valve
d elbow
e pipe support
f flow meter
g underground pipeline
h section of pipe

2 Are there any pipes near where you are right now? What do the pipes carry? What size are they?

3 Are there any major pipelines in your country? Can you name some world-famous pipelines?

Reading

Inspection and cleaning

1 Draw a picture of a pipe. What can go wrong? Draw or write three problems.

2 Match the **bold** words with their meaning.

1 **cause** problems   a stop the flow in
2 **reduce** oil flow   b look carefully at
3 **block** the pipeline   c make plans for
4 **inspect** pipes   d make less
5 **design** tools   e make

3 Read the text. Complete the sentences.

1 D_____ reduce the flow of oil.

2 PSG makes t_____ that clean pipes.

3 Workers use a l_____ to put the device in the pipe.

4 The device has d_____ and b_____. They clean the pipe.

5 Workers take the device out at the r_____.

6 A q_____ is a price for a job.

4 What cleaning jobs do you do in your everyday life? What cleaning tools do you use?

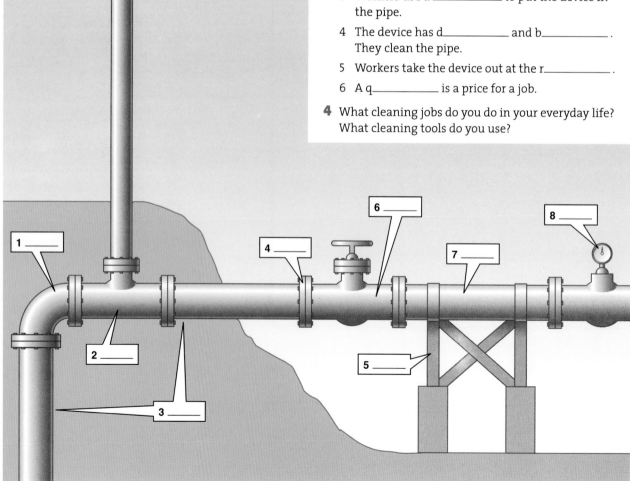

In this unit
- inspection and cleaning
- describing the location of a pipeline
- welding hazards and precautions
- countable and uncountable nouns
- measuring pipes
- isometrics and MTOs

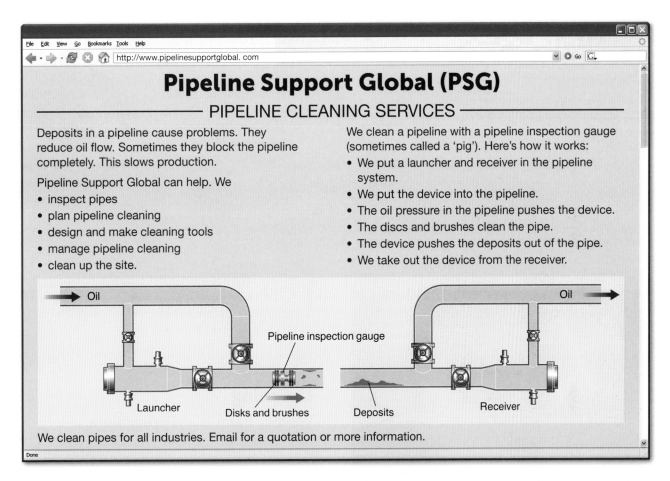

File Edit View Go Bookmarks Tools Help

http://www.pipelinesupportglobal. com

Pipeline Support Global (PSG)
──────── PIPELINE CLEANING SERVICES ────────

Deposits in a pipeline cause problems. They reduce oil flow. Sometimes they block the pipeline completely. This slows production.

Pipeline Support Global can help. We
- inspect pipes
- plan pipeline cleaning
- design and make cleaning tools
- manage pipeline cleaning
- clean up the site.

We clean a pipeline with a pipeline inspection gauge (sometimes called a 'pig'). Here's how it works:
- We put a launcher and receiver in the pipeline system.
- We put the device into the pipeline.
- The oil pressure in the pipeline pushes the device.
- The discs and brushes clean the pipe.
- The device pushes the deposits out of the pipe.
- We take out the device from the receiver.

Oil

Oil

Pipeline inspection gauge

Launcher

Disks and brushes

Deposits

Receiver

We clean pipes for all industries. Email for a quotation or more information.

Done

Speaking
Describing a pipeline

1 Match the descriptions with the numbers on the map.

a At the motorway, the pipe goes underground.
b There's a flow meter just before the pipeline goes into the forest.
c There's an elbow, then the pipeline goes east.
d There's a valve near the tee.
e There's one section of pipe over the river.
f There are two straight sections joined by a flanged joint.
g There are two pipe supports under this section.
h The pipeline goes south for about 100 metres. Then there's a tee.

2 Work in pairs. Student A, go to p.108. Student B, go to p.112.

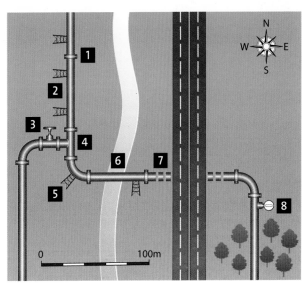

melt (v) to become or make sth liquid as a result of heating

ethanol (n) ethyl alcohol, often made from plants, and then used as biofuel – it can be added to petrol / gasoline

insulate (v) to protect sth with a material that prevents heat, sound, electricity, etc. from passing through

Vocabulary

Welding

Read the text and look at the picture. Answer the questions.

1 What problems can arc rays cause?
2 What problems can smoke cause?
3 What problems can sparks cause?
4 Why is leather good for protection?
5 What do welders wear to protect their faces?

Welding is joining two pieces of metal together by making them very hot. One type of welding machine uses electricity to make a very hot spark called an arc. The arc **melts** the pieces of metal and they join together. Welding makes smoke, sparks, and a type of light called arc rays.

welding helmet
smoke
arc
arc rays
gloves
sparks

Welding hazards
- Sparks can cause fires.
- The electricity that makes the arc can also shock or burn you.
- Arc rays can burn skin (like sunburn) and eyes.
- Smoke can hurt your eyes, nose, and mouth. It can also cause problems with breathing.

Welding protection

Welders wear a helmet that protects their eyes and head. They also wear leather shoes and leather gloves to protect their hands and feet from sparks, arc rays, and hot metal. Leather is made from the skin of animals. It is very strong and it doesn't melt.

It's my job

João Santos – welder

1 🎧 Listen. Answer the questions.
1 Who does João work closely with?
2 What happens to the pipes before João welds them?
3 Who assembles the pipes after the welding?
4 What do the inspectors do after they inspect the pipes?
5 What three welding hazards does João mention?

2 Number the steps in order.
a Inspectors inspect the pipes.
b Pipe-fitters read the plans.
c Workers paint the pipes.
d Pipe-fitters prepare the pipes and put parts together.
e Pipe-fitters assemble the pipes.
f Welders join the sections of pipe.

3 Would you like to do João's job? Why / why not?

Listening

Welding hazards and precautions

1 Look at the picture. Match the names with the parts.
a gas cylinder   d cylinder cap
b valve   e cart
c regulator

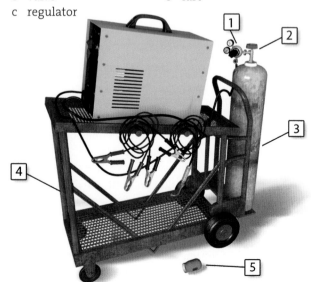

2 Match each sign with a warning.

1 Don't drop the cylinder!
2 Be careful. Don't trip and fall.
3 Secure the gas cylinder.
4 This could explode.
5 Use the ventilation fan.

3 🎧 Listen to the health and safety officer talking to a team of welders and pipe-fitters. Number the welding hazards in the order you hear them.

a gas cylinders   d smoke
b arc sparks   e electric shock
c arc rays   f trips and falls

4 Match each hazard (a–f) in **3** above with a precaution.

1 Weld dry.
2 Always move it safely.
3 Cover up skin and eyes.
4 No pockets!
5 Know the material we're welding.
6 Keep the work area clean and tidy.

5 🎧 Listen again. Tick (✓) the pieces of safety equipment you hear.

1 safety glasses ☐   7 respirator ☐
2 welder's helmet ☐   8 boots ☐
3 face guard ☐   9 ventilation system ☐
4 gloves ☐   10 ear protectors ☐
5 cotton trousers ☐   11 safety harness ☐
6 welding jacket ☐   12 leather shoes ☐

6 What safety precautions do you take when you drive a car, or ride a motorcycle or bicycle?

● **Language spot**

Countable and uncountable nouns

Most nouns have singular and plural forms.

cylinder – cylinders, spark – sparks, material – materials

We call these countable nouns. We can use *a*, *some*, *the*, and *many* with countable nouns.

I have a cylinder.
I see some sparks.
We need the material.
How many cylinders are there?

Some nouns have only one form.

smoke, skin, water

We call these uncountable nouns. We do not use *a / an* or *one, two, three* etc. before uncountable nouns. We use *some* and *much*.

There's some water on the floor.
How much oxygen have we got?

≫ Go to **Grammar reference** p.121

1 Choose the correct words to complete each sentence.

1 We switch off *equipment / an equipment*.
2 There are six main *hazard / hazards* for welders.
3 Gas *cylinder / cylinders* can explode.
4 Never look at *spark / the spark*.
5 Hot sparks can burn *clothes / a clothes* and start fires.
6 *Smoke / A smoke* from welding can be dangerous.
7 Use *cart / a cart*.
8 We always know *material / the material* we're welding.
9 Cover *skin / a skin* and eyes.
10 Don't stand in *water / a water*.

2 Use the words in the list to complete the sentences. Then tick (✓) U (uncountable) or C (countable).

brush   deposits   ethanol   eyes
information   oil   shock   smoke
steam   welder

	U	C
1 Boiling water makes _____ .	☐	☐
2 I have some _____ .	☐	☐
3 I had wet feet and got a _____ .	☐	☐
4 The _____ cleans the pipe.	☐	☐
5 My car holds five litres of _____ .	☐	☐
6 The arc ray burned my _____ .	☐	☐
7 I work as a _____ in Brazil.	☐	☐
8 Don't breathe the _____ !	☐	☐
9 There are some _____ in the pipe.	☐	☐
10 _____ is a biofuel.	☐	☐

3 Complete the sentences with *much* or *many*.

1 How _____ oxygen cylinders are there?
2 How _____ petrol is there?
3 We can't weld here. There's too _____ water on the floor.
4 We have 100 nuts and 200 bolts. There are too _____ bolts!
5 How _____ time have we got?
6 There are eight of us. That's too _____ people for one truck.

Number talk

Measuring pipes

1 Use the words to complete the text.

diameter   inside   length   radius   thickness

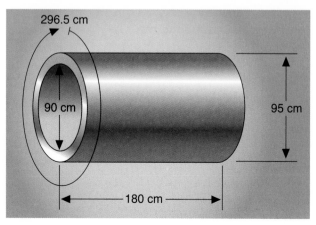

C = circumference
D = outside _____ [1]
B = _____ [2] diameter (bore)
S = pipe wall _____ [3]
L = _____ [4]
r = inside _____ [5] (B / 2)

$$V = \pi r^2 \times L$$

(*Volume equals pi r squared times length.*)

- V = volume (the amount of fluid a pipe can hold)
- π = 3.141 (pronounced *pi*)
- r^2 = radius squared (r × r)

2 Read the formula and the notes. Write and do the calculations. Remember to convert all measurements to metres.

EXAMPLE
L = 12 m, r = 0.5 m. V = _____ m³
We write
3.14 x 0.5 x 0.5 x 12 = 9.42 m³
We say
Three point one four times point five times point five times twelve equals nine point four two cubic metres.

1 L = 12.4 m, r = 22 mm.   V = _____ m³
2 L = 565 m, r = 550 mm.   V = _____ m³
3 L = 22.3 km, r = 1.2 m.   V = _____ m³
4 L = 640 km, r = 1.8 m.   V = _____ m³

3 🎧 Listen and check your answers.

4 Practise saying calculations. Student A, go to p.108. Student B, go to p.113.

5 🎧 Listen and check your answers.

6 Look at the picture in **1**. Answer the questions about the pipe.

1   How long is it?
2   How thick is the wall?
3   What's the bore?
4   What's the outside diameter?
5   What's the pipe's circumference?
6   What is its volume?

Reading

Isometrics and MTOs

1 Read the text. Then look at the drawing and write T (true) or F (false) for each sentence.

Special piping drawings called isometrics show the pipe in three dimensions (height, width, depth) on a flat drawing. The isometric drawing also includes a Material Take Off or MTO which is a list of the material and the parts for a pipeline.

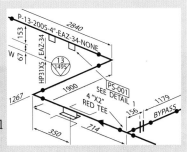

1 This drawing is a list of materials.
2 The drawing shows one tee.
3 2840 mm is probably the pipe's radius.
4 1900 mm is the measurement between the two elbows.
5 The drawing shows calculations for the volume of each pipe section.

2 Look at the table. Use the words in the list to complete the sentences.

	SIZE	DESCRIPTION	MAT. CODE	TOTAL
PIPE	4"	SCH 40		8.0 M
	3"	SCH 40		0.3 M
	2"	SCH 80		2.8 M
VALVES	1"	150# RF FLDG GATE		3
	3"	150# RF FLDG GATE		1
	4"	150# RF FLDG GATE		1
ELBOWS	2"	90° BW LR SCH 80		2
	2"	45° BW LR SCH 80		1
	4"	90° BW LR SCH 40		4

elbow   parts   quantity   sizes   valve

1 The words on the left side are pipeline _____ .
2 90° BW LR SCH 80 is a type of _____ .
3 150# RF FLGD GATE is a type of _____ .
4 1", 2", 4", etc. are _____ .
5 The column on the right shows the _____ for each part, which means how much or how many of each part is needed.

8 Working offshore

Kick off

1 This production platform off the coast of Canada is one of the biggest platforms in the world. Answer the questions.

1 Where can helicopters land on the platform?
2 Where do the workers eat and sleep?
3 How can they escape in an emergency?
4 Which part of the platform processes crude oil?
5 Where do they burn gas if there is too much gas?

2 Which are the three biggest hazards on a platform, and why? Give your opinion.

- flammable gas
- bad weather
- electrical equipment
- sparks
- big waves
- million-tonne icebergs
- other things

Reading

A production platform

1 Match this information with sentences in the text.

1 Nobody can visit an offshore platform without some safety training.
2 Offshore workers must be physically fit.
3 The platform is the same size as a football field.
4 Drilling platforms are smaller than production platforms.
5 The process area separates oil from gas and water.
6 The utilities area provides electricity.

2 Match words from the text with these definitions. The first letter is given.

1 teaching or learning a skill – t_____
2 a number of lessons – c_____
3 part of a place or building – a_____
4 a place to sleep and eat – a_____
5 the area and equipment at the top of a well – w_____
6 services that most buildings have, like electricity and water for example – u_____
7 a machine for making electricity – g_____
8 sending fresh air into and around a building – v_____
9 sending something to many places – d_____

In this unit
- vocabulary for offshore platforms, variables and units of measurement, electrical circuits, radiotelephony
- comparing things positively, negatively, and equally
- how to complete a leave request form
- how to use two-way radios
- how to pronounce consonant clusters

Going offshore

You arrive by helicopter. But first, you receive safety training. Even day visitors must have safety training. Offshore work is more hazardous than onshore work, so workers must also have a medical test and do a fire-fighting and escape course before they go.

You get out of the helicopter and hold on to your hat. You are now standing on a production platform high above the water. It is as big as a football field. The top of the derrick is higher than a twenty-storey building.

Drilling platforms are not as big as this because they only do drilling. Production platforms are bigger because they do more things and must accommodate more people.

A typical production platform has four main areas above the water. One is the accommodation area, where the workers eat and sleep. Another is the well head or drilling area. That contains the derrick, well heads, and drilling equipment. Crude oil comes up to the well heads with gas and water in it. So it goes to the process area, which separates the oil from the other things. All the areas need electricity and other utilities. The utilities area provides these: a generator makes electricity, and there is equipment for heating, ventilation, air conditioning, and water distribution.

3 Circle these prepositions in the text.

Paragraph 1: by, than
Paragraph 2: out of, on to, above, as, of
Paragraph 4: with, in, to, from, for

4 Complete these sentences with a preposition from **3**.

1 Heavy equipment arrives _____ boat.
2 The accommodation area is as big _____ a hotel.
3 Don't get out _____ the helicopter.
4 Hold _____ the rope.
5 The lifeboats are on two sides _____ the platform.
6 What are the cranes _____ ?
7 They are _____ lifting things from boats.
8 The derrick is _____ the well head area.

● Language spot
Comparative sentences

1 Match the phrases with the mathematical symbols.

1 A is bigger than B.
2 A is as big as B.
3 A is not as big as B.

A < B
A > B
A ≈ B

2 🎧 Listen to these four sentences from the text. Notice the rhythm and stress. Practise saying them fluently.

1 Offshore work is more hazardous than onshore work.
2 The platform is as big as a football field.
3 The top of the derrick is higher than a twenty-storey building.
4 Drilling platforms are not as big as this.

3 Compare these things. Use your knowledge and opinions and the adjectives in brackets.

EXAMPLE
boats – helicopters (fast) → *Boats are not as fast as helicopters.*

1 helicopters – boats (fast)
2 crude oil – petrol (heavy)
3 drilling rigs – production platforms (large)
4 safety – speed (important)
5 gas – oil (useful)

4 Some adjectives have irregular comparative forms:

good – better – best   bad – worse – worst

Compare these things. Give your own opinions.

EXAMPLE
physical work – office-based work → *Office-based work is better than physical work.*

1 very cold weather – very hot weather
2 nice work – good pay
3 an offshore job – an onshore job

>> Go to **Grammar reference** p.121

Number talk

Measuring and adjusting variables

1 Match these variables with the four gauges.

Variable	Some common measurement units
pressure	1 bar = 100 kilopascals (kPa)
	10 bar = 1 megapascal (mPa)
temperature	degrees Celsius (°C)
level	per cent (%) or metres (m)
flow	cubic metres per minute (m³/min)

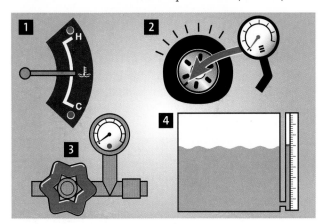

2 Complete these short conversations with the correct variables and units. Then practise saying them.

1 **A** What's the _____ of fluid in this tank?

   B It's 2.1 m. That's 70% full.

2 **A** What's the reading on the _____ gauge?

   B 12 m³/min. Is that lower than usual?

3 **A** The water's hotter than normal. What's the exact _____?

   B The gauge says it's 98 _____.

4 **A** The pump _____ is 24 bar now.

   B It shouldn't be as high as that. It should be 2mPa. That's 20 _____.

3 Give instructions with *Increase* or *Reduce*.

EXAMPLE

15 bar → 20 bar

Increase the pressure to 20 bar.

1 20 bar → 15 bar	4 70% → 95%
2 60 °C → 65 °C	5 2.1 m → 0 m
3 14 m³/min → 10 m³/min	

It's my job

1 Dave Bristow, 22, is an instrument technician. He works on a production platform in the North Sea, off the east coast of the UK.

1 Which instruments do you think Dave uses?

2 Can you explain these verbs?
   adjust   diagnose   inspect   install
   maintain   repair   solve   test

3 Do you think Dave does all these things?

2 🎧 Listen to part 1 and check your answers to **1**.

3 🎧 In part 2, Dave talks about life on the platform. Listen and complete the information. Use these words and numbers:

books   comfortable   good   gym   small
TV   12   7   2

● weeks on and weeks off: _____ᵃ on, _____ᵇ off

● working hours per day: _____ᶜ

● working days per week: _____ᵈ

● free time: _____ᵉ, _____ᶠ, _____ᵍ

● accommodation: _____ʰ, _____ⁱ

● food: _____ʲ

4 Dave says 'For me, it's better than onshore work.' Discuss the questions.

1 What are the advantages and disadvantages of offshore work?

2 Would you like Dave's job? Why / why not?

electricity (noun)
electric / electrical / electronic (adjectives)

Vocabulary
Electricity and circuits

This is a multimeter. Dave uses it to test electrical circuits and measure these variables.

Variables	Units
current (I)	amps (A)
resistance (R)	ohms (Ω)
voltage (V)	volts (V)

1 How are these equations useful? Give examples.
$$V = IR \qquad I = V/R \qquad R = V/I$$

2 Look at the *circuits* a, b, c and d. Match these components with the symbols.

battery   buzzer   cell   lamp   motor
on-off switch   push switch   wire

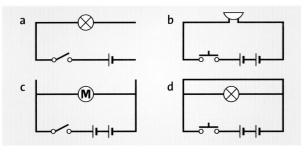

3 Describe each circuit above. Can the circuit work or not? Say why. (A circuit must be *complete* and have no *short circuits*.)

4 Match the descriptions with the correct circuits.
1   a cell, a switch, and two lamps in parallel
2   a cell, a switch, and two lamps in series

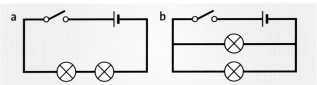

If one lamp fails in the series circuit and in the parallel circuit, what happens to the other lamps? Why?

5 Work in pairs. Draw a circuit. Do not show anyone. Student A, describe your circuit. Student B, listen and draw your partner's circuit. Then swap roles.

Writing
A leave request form

1 Read the information and the form. Then answer the questions.

> Dave (see *It's my job*) has a cousin, Dan. Dan is getting married next Saturday. Dave should work that day, but he wants to go to the wedding. So he must request leave. He must complete this form and give it to the supervisor of the Maintenance crew (name: Martin Olsen).

Leave request form

Employee name	
Department	
Supervisor	

Type of absence requested (please tick one):
❑ Sick
❑ Personal Leave
❑ Maternity / Paternity
❑ Other

Dates of absence
From _____ to _____

Reasons for absence:
_____
_____
_____

Employee's signature _____
Date _____

1   What should Dave write in the *department* box?
    a Production
    b Maintenance
    c Transport
2   Which word means 'not being at work'?
3   Which type of absence should he request?
4   What are the dates for next Saturday and Sunday?
5   What can he write in the *reasons* box?

2 Complete the form for Dave.

Listening

Radio conversation

1 Read about using two-way radios. Then discuss the questions.

- Most two-way radios have a PTT (Press-to-talk) button. Press it and talk. Then say 'Over' and release the button.
- Words can be difficult to hear. So speak clearly in short sentences. People often use easy-to-hear words like *Negative* (No) and *Affirmative* (Yes).

1 How is using a radio different from using a phone?
2 Why are words sometimes difficult to hear?

2 🎧 Listen to a radio conversation between two offshore workers: Martin in the control room and Dave, a technician. Underline the correct words.

1 Dave is in the *process* / *well head* / *utilities* area.
2 Dave must find gauge *P324* / *BD24* / *PD24*.
3 The reading on the gauge is *3* / *5* / *9* bar.
4 The reading in the control room is *higher* / *lower* / *the same*.
5 *Dave* / *Martin* / *They* will diagnose the problem.

3 🎧 Listen again for these phrases. Then say what they mean.

Managing the conversation	Understanding and responding
1 This is (Name).	1 Affirmative
2 (Name.) Do you read?	2 Negative.
3 Go ahead (Name).	3 Say again.
4 Stand by.	4 That's correct.
5 Out.	5 Check.

4 Work in pairs. Practise the conversation on p.128.

Vocabulary

The international radio alphabet

We often need to spell out words, names, and codes on the radio and the phone. Some letters are difficult to hear correctly, for example P, B, V, and E. The international spelling alphabet solves this problem.

1 🎧 Listen and repeat.

A	Alpha		N	November
B	Bravo		O	Oscar
C	Charlie		P	Papa
D	Delta		Q	Quebec
E	Echo		R	Romeo
F	Foxtrot		S	Sierra
G	Golf		T	Tango
H	Hotel		U	Uniform
I	India		V	Victor
J	Juliet		W	Whiskey
K	Kilo		X	X-Ray
L	Lima		Y	Yankee
M	Mike		Z	Zulu

Br E	Am E
zed	zee

2 You don't need to understand the words, but it may help you to remember them. Find

1 people (9)
2 countries and cities (3)
3 letters from the Greek alphabet (2)
4 dances (2)
5 a sport
6 a building
7 a month
8 a weight
9 reflected sound
10 light waves
11 clothes
12 a drink
13 a Spanish word for mountains
14 an exclamation: 'Well done!'

3 🎧 Listen and complete.

1 Employee name: _____

2 Part number: _____

3 Building: _____

4 Web address: _____

4 Spell these items clearly using the radio alphabet.

1 Part nos: B20 and P24

2 Company name: AFS

3 Employee name: Vazy

4 helicopter no. G-CAND

Speaking

Radio conversations

1 Look again at the phrases in *Listening* **3**.

2 Now work in pairs. Student A, go to p.108. Student B, go to p.113.

Pronunciation

Clusters are groups of consonants, such as *str, ct, xtr*. They can be difficult to pronounce correctly.

1 🎧 Listen to these words. Notice the sounds in the red parts. Tick (✓) the true sentences.

There are no extra sounds between the red letters. ☐

Some of the red letters sound weaker than normal. ☐

1 instrument	5 foxtrot	9 install
2 inspect	6 offshore	10 equipment
3 platform	7 production	11 volts
4 stand by	8 electric	12 department

2 🎧 Listen again and repeat the words.

3 Work in pairs. Practise these phrases.

1 an offshore production platform

2 Stand by, Foxtrot One.

3 It's an electrical instrument.

4 I'll install the equipment.

5 fifty volts or sixty volts

Checklist

Assess your progress in this unit. Tick (✓) the statements which are true.

☐ I know some key words connected with working offshore

☐ I can make positive, negative, and equal comparative sentences

☐ I can talk about measurement and adjustment of variables

☐ I can talk about electrical circuits

☐ I can complete a leave request form

☐ I can understand and use language for radio communications

☐ I can pronounce consonant clusters correctly

Key words

Nouns
area
circuit
gauge
instrument
level
platform
pressure
training
variable
well head
wire

Verbs
adjust
go ahead
increase
stand by

Look back through this unit. Find five more words or expressions that you think are useful.

Writing bank

1 Notes

1 Match the halves of the notes.

1 _____ These are the wrong bolts.

2 _____ Please return 9 of these screwdrivers.

3 _____ This electric drill is broken.

a We need 1, not 10!

b We need a new one.

c We need 20 PD798. These are 20 PD790.

2 Match each note in **1** with a picture.

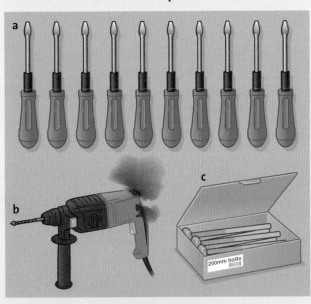

3 Look at the packing list and the picture. There are three problems. Write three short notes.

Packing list

Number	Item	Comments
100	M10 BZP hex nuts	received M12
100	5.5 x 45mm SD screws	1,000 in box

4 Complete the notes using the words in the list.
afternoon   July   return   this morning

1 Rob phoned at nine o'clock _____ . Please call him (0772–6889) as soon as possible.

2 I'm at lunch. I will _____ at 2.30.

3 Can we meet on Wednesday the 25th of _____ ?

4 I'm in Dubai until Tuesday _____ .

Writing tips: abbreviations

For days and months, we can write the first three letters.

Jul = July   Sun = Sunday
Jan = January   Fri = Friday

Other useful abbreviations are
rtn = return
pls = please
asap = as soon as possible (quickly)
a.m. = in the morning
p.m. = in the afternoon / evening

---

5 Read the notes. Match the short words 1–8 with their meanings a–h.

> Rob phoned 9 a.m.[1]
> Pls[2] call 0772–6889
> asap[3]

> At lunch.
> Will rtn[4] 2.30.

> Can we meet on
> Wed[5] 25 Jul[6]?

> In Dubai until
> Tue[7] p.m.[8]

a please   e return
b as soon as possible   f in the afternoon / evening
c Tuesday   g in the morning
d Wednesday   h July

6 Write notes with abbreviations.

1 We need a new drill quickly.
2 I will return on Friday 21 August.
3 Please order 20 PD798 for next Tuesday.
4 Abdullah phoned at 3.00 this afternoon.
5 I'm in the workshop and will return at 10.00.

2 An informal email asking for information

1 Complete the emails. Use the words in the list.

Are   Do   Does   Is

1

| File | Edit | View | Tools | Message | Help |

Sami,
_____ you have Paul's new email address?
Thanks!
Reem

2

| File | Edit | View | Tools | Message | Help |

Mr Ping,
_____ the Shanghai office open on Wednesday?
Piet Donkerloot

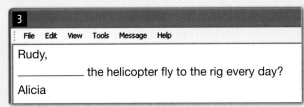

3

| File | Edit | View | Tools | Message | Help |

Rudy,
_____ the helicopter fly to the rig every day?
Alicia

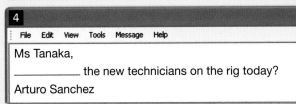

4

| File | Edit | View | Tools | Message | Help |

Ms Tanaka,
_____ the new technicians on the rig today?
Arturo Sanchez

2 Match each reply below with a message in **1**.
  a No, it isn't.
  b Yes, they are.
  c No, sorry, I don't. I'll ask Suresh for it.
  d Yes, it does, except when the weather's bad.

3 Complete the sentences with a name from **1**.
  1 _____ receives an email from Reem.
  2 _____ asks about the Shanghai office.
  3 _____ receives an email from Alicia.
  4 _____ asks about the new technicians.
  5 _____ wants Paul's email address.
  6 _____ receives an email from Arturo.
  7 _____ receives an email from Piet.
  8 _____ asks about the helicopter.

Writing tips: names in emails

In an informal email, begin with the name of the person you're writing to. This may be a first name or a family name with a title.

Mr = any man
Mrs = a married woman
Miss = a girl or an unmarried woman
Ms = any woman
Dr = doctor

In English, we
- don't use a title with a first name
- don't use a family name without a title.

Put your name at the bottom of an email.
- Don't use a title when you write your own name.
- In a message that begins with the person's first name, end with your own first name.
- In a message to Mr, Mrs, Dr, etc. write your own first name and last name.

4 Match the halves of the emails.

1 ☐
Dr Sipkowski,
I've hurt my arm.

2 ☐
Bernie,
I want to talk to you about my laptop.

3 ☐
Ms Lim
I have some letters to send.

a
Are you working in the control room today?
Adam

b
Are you going to the post office today?
Angelo Marcos

c
Are you working in the clinic today?
Wolfgang Schiffer

5 Write short emails.
  1 Ask Ali: Murat's telephone number?
  2 Ask Ms Oi: the Kuala Lumpur office open on Monday?
  3 Ask Russell: supplies come every week?
  4 Ask Mr Carlson: new manager in the office today?

3 An email reporting an IT problem

1 Read the email. What problem is Lucy King having?

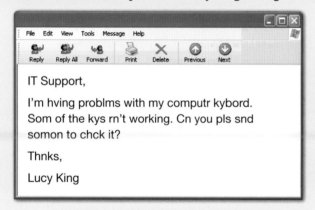

File   Edit   View   Tools   Message   Help

Reply   Reply All   Forward   Print   Delete   Previous   Next

IT Support,

I'm hving problms with my computr kybord.
Som of the kys rn't working. Cn you pls snd
somon to chck it?

Thnks,

Lucy King

2 Which two keys on her keyboard aren't working?

3 Correct the spelling of the words with missing letters.

4 Match each sentence with a picture.

1   I'm having problems with my printer.
2   There's a problem with my hand-held computer.
3   There's a problem with my laptop computer.
4   I'm having trouble with my desktop computer.
5   I'm having problems with my external hard drive.

5 Use the words to complete the sentences.

flashing   getting   making   showing
working

1   The red light is _____ .
2   The plug is _____ very hot.
3   The keypad isn't _____ properly.
4   The screen is _____ an error message.
5   It's _____ a funny noise when it prints.

6 Match each sentence in **5** with a picture in **4**.

Writing tips: explaining IT problems

- If you don't know the name of the person, address the message to the department.
- Say the equipment you're having a problem with.
- Say exactly what the problem is.
- Say what you want or need.
- Say 'thank you'.
- Write your name at the end of the message.

---

7 Number the parts of the email in the correct order.

a   Could you send someone to check it?
b   IT Support,
c   Mary Wong
d   Thank you.
e   The screen isn't working.
f   There's a problem with my laptop computer.

8 Write an email to IT Support about each of these problems.

1   desktop computer – making strange noise
2   mouse – button not working properly
3   laptop computer screen – going off and on
4   hand-held computer – showing an error message
5   printer – red light flashing

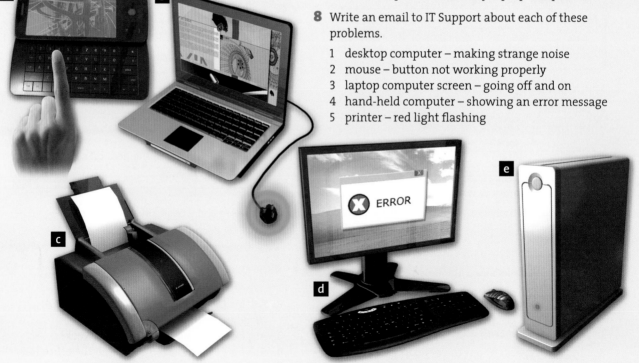

4 An email making an IT request

1 Match the halves of the email messages.

1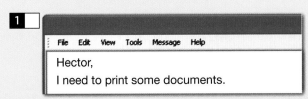

File Edit View Tools Message Help

Hector,
I need to print some documents.

2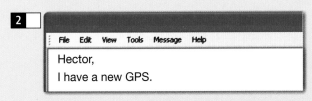

File Edit View Tools Message Help

Hector,
I have a new GPS.

3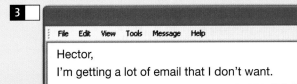

File Edit View Tools Message Help

Hector,
I'm getting a lot of email that I don't want.

4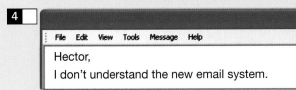

File Edit View Tools Message Help

Hector,
I don't understand the new email system.

a Could you please give me a new email
address?
Thanks.
Marta

b Could you please show me how to connect
my laptop to the printer?
Thank you.
Ian

c Could you please help me put the maps in it?
Thanks.
Ralph

d Could you please explain how it works?
Thank you!
Jo

2 Choose the correct word to complete each sentence.

1 I need Khaled's *email address / password* to send
him a message.
2 I need new *maps / documents* on my GPS.
3 I want to use the *printer / email system* to send and
receive messages.
4 My old *email address / password* is ky58s0.
5 I want to use my new computer to write letters and
to make forms and other *maps / documents*.
6 We need more paper for the *printer / email system*.

3 Complete the sentences. Use the words in the list.

change   explain   give   help   put   show

1 Could you please _____ me a new email
password?
2 Could you please _____ me connect my
laptop to the internet?
3 Could you please _____ me how to use my
new computer?
4 Could you please _____ the new maps on my
GPS?
5 Could you please _____ how I can use the
wireless network?
6 Could you please _____ my email address?

Writing tips: making a request

- If you know the person's name, begin the
message with it.
- Say why you are making a request.
- Make the request.
- Say 'thank you'.
- Write your name at the end of the message.

---

4 Write emails to Hector in IT. Make requests.

1 You have a new GPS. You want to connect it to your
laptop.
2 You have a new email address but you don't have
the password.
3 You want to connect your hand-held computer to
the wireless network.
4 You need to print some documents, but you don't
understand the new printer.
5 You have a new computer. You want to connect it to
the internet.

5 Notes with warnings and instructions

1 Match each note with a picture.

1
Please don't destroy these.

2
Please make 16 copies of this for the meeting tomorrow.

3
Please don't remove this from the workshop.

4
Please take this to IT for repair.

5
Please use the stairs.

6
Please put in some petrol.

2 Put the words in the correct order to make notes.
1 office / send / letter / this / please / the / to / Bahrain
2 don't / computer / this / use / please
3 this / to / safety / the / officer / please / take / key
4 don't / please / these / drawings / from / workshop / the / remove
5 copies / please / 10 / this / of / make / letter
6 don't / this / destroy / please / drawing

3 Complete the notes with *from*, *to*, *of*, or *X* (no word needed).
1 Please don't remove this _____ my desk.
2 Please take this _____ the control room.
3 Please don't use _____ this.
4 Please make five copies _____ these.
5 Please don't destroy _____ this.
6 Please send this _____ Andres Valentino.

> **Writing tips: *this* and *these***
>
> - When a note is attached to a single thing, you use *this*. For example *Please don't remove this book from the workshop.*
> - When a note is attached to more than one thing, you use *these*. For example *Please don't destroy these drawings.*

4 Write short notes.
1 You have some old documents. You want them to be destroyed.
2 You have a laptop computer. You don't want anyone to remove it from the office.
3 The printer isn't working properly. You don't want anyone to use it.
4 You have an instruction manual for a power tool. You want someone to take it to the workshop.
5 You have a letter. You want someone to send it to the Jakarta office.
6 You have some documents. You want someone to make ten copies of them.
7 You have some drawings. You don't want anyone to destroy them.
8 You have some plans. You don't want anyone to copy them.
9 You have two new radios. You don't want anyone to use them.
10 You don't understand a note that someone has written. You want someone to explain it to you.

6 An email asking for leave

1 Read the emails. Match the meanings a–e with the underlined words.

a a high body temperature because you are ill
b time away from work because you are ill
c an event where a man and a woman become husband and wife
d time away from work because of something unexpected
e time away from work for holiday

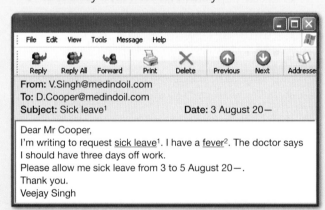

From: V.Singh@medindoil.com
To: D.Cooper@medindoil.com
Subject: Sick leave[1]   Date: 3 August 20—

Dear Mr Cooper,
I'm writing to request <u>sick leave</u>[1]. I have a <u>fever</u>[2]. The doctor says I should have three days off work.
Please allow me sick leave from 3 to 5 August 20—.
Thank you.
Veejay Singh

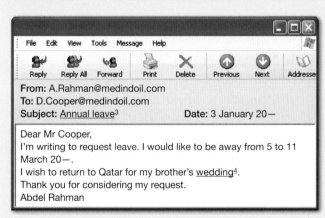

From: A.Rahman@medindoil.com
To: D.Cooper@medindoil.com
Subject: <u>Annual leave</u>[3]   Date: 3 January 20—

Dear Mr Cooper,
I'm writing to request leave. I would like to be away from 5 to 11 March 20—.
I wish to return to Qatar for my brother's <u>wedding</u>[4].
Thank you for considering my request.
Abdel Rahman

From: Rudy.Batao@medindoil.com
To: D.Cooper@medindoil.com
Subject: Emergency leave   Date: 31 May 20—

Dear Mr Cooper,
I'm writing to request <u>emergency leave</u>[5]. My father is very ill. I wish to return to Manila immediately.
Please allow me emergency leave from 1 to 8 June 20—.
Thank you.
Rudy Batao

2 Read the emails and answer the questions.

1 Which worker is ill now?
2 Whose father is ill?
3 Who is going to an important family event?
4 How many days will Abu Rahman be away?
5 Who asks for leave two months from now?
6 Who asks for leave starting tomorrow?

3 Match the sentence halves.

1 I have   a brother is very ill.
2 I'm going to   b I should rest.
3 My   c in hospital.
4 My mother is   d a high fever.
5 My sister   e is getting married.
6 The doctor says   f Rio de Janeiro with my wife.

4 What kind of leave is each sentence in **3** about? Write A (annual leave), S (sick leave), or E (emergency leave).

Writing tips: asking for time off

- Say what type of leave you are asking for.
- Say the reason you are requesting leave.
- Give the dates you wish to be away.
- Say thank you.

5 Write three emails requesting leave.

1 You want to go to your sister's wedding. You want leave from 8 to 15 May.
2 You have hurt your hand. The doctor says you should have five days off work, from 6 to 10 September.
3 Your son is ill. You wish to return home from 10 to 16 December.

7 A service report

1 Match the words with the definitions.

1	client	a	a person who services and maintains machinery
2	technician	b	a person or company who receives a service
3	contact	c	at a company, the person who is responsible for talking to people outside the company about a certain job

2 Read the service report. Write T (true) or F (false).

1 The discharge hose was damaged.
2 There was a problem with a valve.
3 The technician repaired the hose.
4 The technician replaced the valve.
5 The technician finished the job.
6 The equipment now works properly.
7 Power Products is the client.

Power Products
SERVICE REPORT

Oak Street Farstow Kent Tel: 446-7230	Date 5 Feb Site BR Farstow Refinery Request No 513

Client Bay Refinoil
Address King Industrial Estate, Farstow
Contact Jim Purley
Tel 337–2901

Description
Leaky valve on discharge hose in bulk tanker loading area bay 3.
Valve damaged.
Replaced valve.
Working OK.

Start time: 8.15 Finish time: 10.30
Technician: Phil Jones
Client signature: *Jim Purley*

---

3 Complete the technician's description of the job.

There was a _____ _____[1] on the discharge hose in the _____ _____ _____ _____[2], bay 3. The valve was _____[3]. I replaced the _____[4]. Now it's _____[5] OK.

Writing tips: a service report

- Say what isn't working.
- Say what the problem was.
- Say what you did.
- Say if the problem is now solved.

---

4 Read the technician's description of another job. Complete the service report.

On 4 April, I went to BR's well head at Tophill at 10.00 a.m. The portable screw compressor had low pressure and was making a lot of noise. The service valve gasket was damaged. I replaced the service valve gasket. I checked the pressure and added oil. Now it's working OK. I left the site at 12.30 p.m.

Power Products
SERVICE REPORT

Oak Street Farstow Kent Tel: 446-7230	Date _____[1] Site _____[2] Request No 514

Client Bay Refinoil
Address King Industrial Estate, Farstow
Contact Jim Purley
Tel 3372901

Description
_____
_____[3]
_____[4]
_____[5]
_____[6]

Start time: _____[7] Finish time: _____[8]
Technician: Phil Jones
Client signature: *Jim Purley*

8 An equipment damage report

1 Look at the picture. Read the email. Answer the questions.

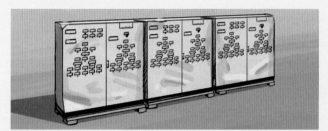

> John,
>
> We need to install some new control cabinets, but they're damaged. We can't use them. They were delivered on 17 July and they were accepted. They're in Warehouse 4. Could you inspect them, please? We need these on 30 November.
>
> Thanks.
>
> Bill Hayes

1 Have the control cabinets been installed?
2 What's the problem with the cabinets?
3 Where are the cabinets?
4 What does Bill ask John to do?

2 Complete the equipment damage report. Use the words in the list.

delivered	dented	inspect	reported
scratched	stored		

> To: Clive Buckley, Procurement Manager
> From: John Battersby, Inspector
> Date: 9 Sep 20—
> Subject: Delivery Damage Report
> Notes: The Construction Department _____1 damage to control cabinets in Warehouse 4 and asked me to _____2 the damage. The cabinets were _____3 on 17 Jul and accepted.
> Damage: The cabinets are _____4 and the paintwork is _____5.
> Probable cause: The cabinets were _____6 on a busy corner in the warehouse. Possible fork-lift collision.
> Recommendation: Replace. Construction Department needs the cabinets on 30 Nov 20—.

3 Match each probable cause of damage with a picture.

1 They were scratched and dented before they were delivered to us.
2 They were dropped from a fork-lift.
3 They were damaged by a fork-lift collision.

> ### Writing tips: an equipment damage report
>
> An equipment damage report includes
> - the piece of equipment that is damaged
> - a description of the damage
> - information about the cause of the damage
> - a recommendation (usually return it, repair it, or replace it).

4 Read the email. Complete the information for an equipment damage report.

> File Edit View Tools Message Help
>
> John,
>
> We need to install a new cooling unit, but it's damaged. It was delivered on 10 August and it was accepted, but it was dropped from a fork-lift. The cover is bent. It's in Warehouse 2. Could you inspect it, please? I think we can repair it. We need it on 20 December.
>
> Thanks.
>
> Bill Hayes

> To: Clive Buckley, Procurement Manager
> From: John Battersby, Inspector
> Date: 11 Oct 20—
> Subject: Delivery Damage Report
> Notes: _____1
> Damage: _____2
> Probable cause: _____3
> Recommendation: _____4

9 A shift handover log

1 Read about shift work. Complete the sentences.

The oil and gas industry works 24 hours a day, seven days a week. The 24-hour day is divided into two shifts of twelve hours or three shifts of eight hours. When one shift finishes and the next begins, the workers must communicate clearly. They write in a book called a log. They explain the work they have finished and the work that they haven't finished.

1 A _____ is usually eight or twelve hours long.

2 Workers write in a book called a _____ .

3 They write about _____ they have and haven't completed.

2 Read the shift handover log. Choose the correct words in each sentence below.

Shift handover log	
Date: 27 March 20– Time: 17.30	
Work completed	
Job card	Task
E2095	Installation of new pump at CC1467 (jetty)
E2096	Checking emergency lighting in Warehouse 5
E2083	200-hour maintenance on generator P1023A (welders' portable)
Work not completed	
Job card	Task
E2100	Installation of electrical wiring to new control cabinets in control room (H108). Materials collected and checked. Risk assessment complete. Installation ongoing.
E2102	Checking fire extinguishers in admin block.
Notes Darren reported sick. Won't be in until Wednesday.	

1 They *have / haven't* installed the new pump.

2 They *are checking / have checked* the emergency lighting.

3 The generator maintenance *is / isn't* finished.

4 They have *started / finished* installing the electrical wiring.

5 They *are doing / have done* the risk assessment.

6 They *have collected / will collect* the materials.

7 They *have / haven't* checked the fire extinguishers.

8 Darren *was / wasn't* at work today.

Writing tips: a shift handover log

- We say
  We've installed the new pump.
  We've checked the emergency lighting.
  We need to install the wiring.
  We need to check the fire extinguishers.

- We write
  Work completed
  installation of new pump
  checking emergency lighting
  Work outstanding
  installation of wiring
  checking fire extinguishers

3 Read the workshop manager's words. Complete the shift handover log.

We've started job card E4101 – installing new emergency lighting in Warehouse 5. We've collected and checked the materials, but we haven't finished installing the lighting. We've finished the 100-hour maintenance on the pump at CC1467 on the jetty. That's job card E4096. We've also changed the leads on the welders' portable generator, P1023A. That's job card E4095. We haven't done job card E4098. That's the repairs to the damaged electrical wiring in the control room. One more thing. Bill is on leave. He will return next Tuesday.

Shift handover log	
Date: 17 Sep 20– Time: 08.30	
Work completed	
Job card	Task
_____1	_____2
_____3	_____4
Work not completed	
Job card	Task
_____5	_____6
_____7	_____8
Notes	
_____9	

Br E	Am E
queue	line

10 A suggestion

1 Look at the pictures. Answer the questions.

1 What's happening in picture 1?

2 What's happening in picture 2?

2 Use the words to complete the description of the pictures.

desk   form   long   queues   requisition
store   storeman   time   tool   waiting

The storeman works at the _____ _____¹.
Each worker gives him a _____ _____
_____². This is a piece of paper that says what
tools the worker needs. At 10.30, there are _____
_____³. The _____ _____⁴ is
sometimes twenty minutes. At 11.30, the store is quiet
and the _____⁵ is not busy.

3 Read the suggestion form. Choose the best words to complete each sentence.

1 *Peter Ives / The storeman* made this suggestion.

2 He hopes that his suggestion will help workers *save time / be safer*.

3 He suggests changing the *tool requisition form / store hours*.

4 He thinks workers should drop off their *forms / tools* then return later to collect their order.

5 If the system is changed, the storeman will prepare *some / all* of the tools ahead of time

---

SUGGESTION FORM

Name: Peter Ives

Dept: Maintenance   **Date:** April 24 20—

Health & safety ☐   **Efficiency** ☒
Customer relations ☐   **Sales** ☐

Title: Reducing waiting time at tool store

Situation: Sometimes there are long queues at the tool store. At other times the storeman is not busy.

Suggested improvement: Change the tool requisition form to include a pick-up time. It is often possible to order two or three hours ahead. Ask workers to leave their forms in a special box at the store desk and return to pick up their order later.

The storeman can prepare orders when he is less busy. Workers can come to the desk to collect them. This will reduce queuing time.

Signed: Peter Ives

Writing tips: a suggestion

● Explain the situation.
● Explain how to improve it.

4 Look at the situations. Write suggestions.

When the 8.00 shift starts, there are long queues of cars waiting to get in the car park.

People who are leaving the main warehouse are sometimes knocked over by people who are entering.

Writing bank key

1 Notes

1 1 c   2 a   3 b

2 a2   b3   c1

3 (Possible answers)
1 These are the wrong nuts. We need 100 M10 BZP hex nuts, not 100 M12 BZP hex nuts.
2 Please return 900 of these screws. We need 100, not 1000!
3 This wrench is broken. Please order a new one.

4 1 this morning   3 July
2 return   4 afternoon

5 a2   b3   c7   d5   e4   f8   g1   h6

6 1 We need a new drill asap.
2 I will rtn Fri 21 Aug.
3 Pls order 20 PD798 for next Tue.
4 Abdullah phoned at 3.00 p.m.
5 I'm in the workshop and will rtn at 10.00.

2 An informal email asking for information

1 1 Do   3 Does
2 Is   4 Are

2 a2   b4   c1   d3

3 1 Sami   5 Reem
2 Piet Donkerloot   6 Ms Tanaka
3 Rudy   7 Mr Ping
4 Arturo Sanchez   8 Alicia

4 1 c   2 a   3 b

5 (Possible answers)
1 Ali,
Do you have Murat's telephone number?
Thanks!
2 Ms Oi,
Is the Kuala Lumpur office open on Monday?
3 Russell,
Do the supplies come every week?
4 Mr Carlson,
Is the new manager in the office today?

3 An email reporting an IT problem

1 Some of the keys on Lucy King's computer aren't working.

2 The *e* and the *a* keys aren't working.

3 I'm having problems with my computer keyboard. Some of the keys aren't working. Can you please send someone to check it? Thanks,

4 1 c   2 a   3 b   4 d   5 e

5 1 flashing   4 showing
2 getting   5 making
3 working

6 1 e   2 b   3 a   4 d   5 c

7 a4   b1   c6   d5   e3   f2

8 (Possible answers)
1 I'm having problems with my computer. It's making a strange noise. Can you please send someone to check it?
2 There's a problem with my computer. The mouse button isn't working properly. Can you please send someone to check it?
3 I'm having trouble with my laptop computer. The screen is going off and on. Can you please send someone to check it?
4 I'm having problems with my hand-held computer. It's showing an error message. Can you please send someone to check it?
5 There's a problem with my printer. The red light is flashing. Can you please send someone to check it?

4 An email making an IT request

1 1 b   2 c   3 a   4 d

2 1 email address   4 password
2 maps   5 documents
3 email system   6 printer

3 1 give   4 put
2 help   5 explain
3 show   6 change

4 (Possible answers)
1 Hector, I have a new GPS. Could you please help me connect it to my laptop?
2 Hector, I have a new email address, but I don't have the password. Could you please give me a password?
3 Hector, I want to connect my hand-held computer to the wireless network. Could you please explain how to do it?
4 Hector, I need to print some documents, but I don't understand the new printer. Could you please show me how it works?
5 Hector, I have a new computer. I want to connect it to the internet. Could you please help me?

5 Notes with warnings and instructions

1 1 b   2 d   3 c   4 a   5 e   6 f

2 1 Please send this letter to the Bahrain office.
2 Please don't use this computer.
3 Please take this key to the safety officer.
4 Please don't remove these drawings from the workshop.
5 Please make 10 copies of this letter.
6 Please don't destroy this drawing.

3 1 from   4 of
2 to   5 X
3 X   6 to

4 (Possible answers)
1 Please destroy these documents.
2 Please don't remove this computer from the office.
3 Please don't use this printer.
4 Please take this instruction manual to the workshop.
5 Please send this letter to the Jakarta office.
6 Please make ten copies of these documents.
7 Please don't destroy these drawings.

8 Please don't copy these plans.
9 Please don't use these radios.
10 Please explain this note to me.

6 An email asking for leave

1 a2 b1 c4 d5 e3

2 1 Veejay Singh   4 6
2 Rudy Batao   5 Abu Rahman
3 Abdel Rahman   6 Rudy Batao

3 1d 2f 3a 4c 5e 6b

4 1S 2A 3E 4E 5A 6S

5 (Possible answers)
1 I'm writing to request leave. I would like to be away from 8 to 15 May. I wish to return home for my sister's wedding. Thank you for considering my request.
2 I'm writing to request sick leave. I've hurt my hand. The doctor says I should have five days off work. Please allow me sick leave 6 to 10 September. Thank you.
3 I'm writing to request emergency leave. My son is ill. I wish to return home immediately. Please allow me emergency leave from 10 to 16 December. Thank you.

7 A service report

1 1b 2a 3c

2 1F 2T 3T 4T 5T 6T 7F

3 1 leaky valve
2 bulk tanker loading area
3 damaged
4 valve
5 working

4 1 4 April
2 BR Tophill well head
3 Portable screw compressor had low pressure and was making a lot of noise.
4 Service valve gasket damaged.
5 Replaced service valve gasket. Checked pressure and added oil.
6 Working OK.
7 10.00 a.m.
8 12.30 p.m.

8 An equipment damage report

1 1 no
2 They're damaged.
3 in Warehouse 4
4 inspect the cabinets

2 1 reported   4 dented
2 inspect   5 scratched
3 delivered   6 stored

3 1b 2a 3c

4 1 The Construction Department reported damage to a cooling unit in Warehouse 2 and asked me to inspect the damage. The unit was delivered on 10 Aug and was accepted.
2 The cover is bent.
3 It was dropped from a fork-lift.
4 Repair. The Construction Department needs the cooling unit on 20 Dec.

9 A shift handover log

1 1 shift   3 work
2 log

2 1 have   5 have done
2 have checked 6 have collected
3 is   7 haven't
4 started   8 wasn't

3 1 E4096
2 100-hour maintenance on pump CC1467 (jetty).
3 E4095
4 Changing leads on welder's portable generator P1023A.
5 E4101
6 Installation of new emergency lighting in Warehouse 5. Materials collected and checked. Installation ongoing.
7 E4098
8 Repair damaged electrical wiring in control room.
9 Bill is on leave. He'll return next Tuesday.

10 A suggestion

1 1 There are long queues at the tool store. The storeman is very busy.
2 There are no queues at the tool store. The storeman isn't busy.

2 1 store desk
2 tool requisition form
3 long queues
4 waiting time
5 storeman

3 1 Peter Ives
2 save time
3 tool requisition form
4 forms
5 some

4 (possible answers)
1 Title: Reducing car park traffic
Situation: When the 8.00 shift starts, there are long queues of cars waiting to get into the car park.
Suggested improvement: Change the shift start time. It would be possible to have half of the employees start at 7.45 and half start at 8.00. This would reduce the traffic.
2 Title: Making warehouse door safe
Situation: People who are leaving the main warehouse are sometimes knocked over by people entering.
Suggested improvement: Install a window in the warehouse door. People using the door would be able to see each other.

9 Natural gas

Kick off

1 Match sentences 1–5 with pictures a–e.

1 The Tupolev Tu-155 transport aircraft can be powered by Liquefied Natural Gas.
2 Gas-fired power stations generate electricity.
3 Some cities fuel buses with natural gas because it burns cleanly.
4 Homes all over the world use natural gas for cooking and heating.
5 Natural gas is used to make ammonia for fertilizer. Fertilizer is food for plants.

2 Answer the questions.

1 How is power generated in your country?
2 Do you use gas for cooking? How does the gas get to your home?
3 Are there any gas-powered cars or buses in your town or city?
4 What plants do farmers in your country grow?
5 Why is natural gas a good fuel for a plane?

3 Complete the sentences using the list.

NH_3 CH_4 LNG

1 Natural gas is mostly _____ – methane.
2 _____ stands for liquefied natural gas.
3 The chemical symbol for ammonia is _____ .

Vocabulary

Gas production and distribution

1 Complete the table.

verb	noun (process)	noun (substance)
vaporize	vaporization	1
liquefy	liquefaction	2
3	production	product
consume	4	
5	storage	
transport	6	
7	pipe	

2 🎧 Listen and check your answers.

In this unit
- gas production and distribution
- talking about a bar chart
- Past Simple *be*
- the Sakhalin II project
- describing equipment

3 Look at the picture. Use words from **1** to complete the sentences.

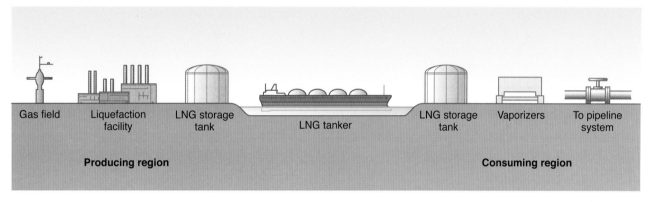

Gas field | Liquefaction facility | LNG storage tank | LNG tanker | LNG storage tank | Vaporizers | To pipeline system

Producing region | **Consuming region**

1 The gas field p_____ gas.
2 It comes out of the ground as a v_____ .
3 The liquefaction facility l_____ the gas.
4 The gas is now a l_____ . It goes into the tanks.
5 The tanks s_____ the gas.
6 Tankers t_____ the liquid gas from the producing region to the consuming region.
7 The gas goes from the tanker into tanks for s_____ .
8 The vaporizers v_____ the gas.
9 The pipeline system p_____ the gas to consumers.
10 Homes, businesses, power stations, and so on c_____ the gas.

4 Look at the picture again. Complete the sentences using the words in the list.

consumption liquefaction pipes product
production transportation vaporization

1 _____ happens in the consuming region.
2 _____ happens between the gas field and the storage tanks.
3 Fertilizer _____ uses natural gas.
4 In the tanker, the _____ is liquid.
5 _____ is the final step in the process.
6 In the picture, a tanker is used for gas _____ .
7 The gas travels to consumers through _____ .

5 How many things can you name for each category?

1 Things that are stored in tanks
2 Things that are transported by ship
3 Things that travel through pipes
4 Things that are produced in one region and consumed in another
5 Things that are sometimes liquid and sometimes vapour

Number talk

Talking about a bar chart

1 Can you say these numbers aloud?

1 1970 (year)
2 2002 (year)
3 1.5 trillion m³
4 2,000,000,000 m³

2 🎧 Listen and check your answers.

3 Look at the chart. Complete the sentences with numbers.

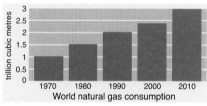

World natural gas consumption

1 2000 consumption was a little less than _____ trillion cubic metres.
2 Consumption in 1970 was _____ m³.
3 1980 consumption was higher than _____ consumption.
4 Consumption in _____ was 2,000,000,000,000 m³.

4 Answer the questions.

1 About how much does consumption increase in ten years?
2 Can you guess 2020 consumption?
3 Can you guess 1960 consumption?

Br E	Am E
holiday	vacation

● Language spot

Past Simple *be*

We use the Past Simple like this:

*Consumption **was** one trillion cubic metres in 1970.*

*They **were** in China last month.*

*We **weren't** busy yesterday.*

*I **wasn't** at work last week.*

***Were** you busy last week?*

***Was** the ship late?*

>> Go to **Grammar reference** p.122

1 Write sentences in the Past Simple.

1 The gas is stored in tanks.

   _____

2 Ahmed isn't late.

   _____

3 She's in Saudi Arabia.

   _____

4 Ian and Matt aren't in the office.

   _____

5 I'm in the workshop.

   _____

6 You aren't in Russia.

   _____

7 We aren't busy.

   _____

8 The gas isn't liquid.

   _____

9 Klaus is in Germany.

   _____

10 She isn't from Qatar.

   _____

2 Make questions in the Past Simple.

1 you / a student / last year ?

   _____

2 your friends / at your house / last week ?

   _____

3 your teacher / at work / last Saturday ?

   _____

4 you and your classmates / at the library / last night ?

   _____

3 Now answer the questions in **2**.

Listening

The past and the present

1 🎧 Listen. Choose the correct word to complete each sentence.

Conversation 1

1 The meeting was *yesterday / this morning*.
2 The new operations manager *was / wasn't* at the meeting.
3 The new operations manager *is / was* at the Ras Tanura refinery.

Conversation 2

4 They *are / were* busy.
5 There *is / was* a big problem.
6 The level gauge *was / wasn't* faulty.

Conversation 3

7 They *are / were* on their way to the warehouse.
8 The cable trays *are / aren't* ready.
9 It *was / wasn't* on the materials report.

2 🎧 Listen again. Check your answers.

3 Number the sentences. 1 = now, 8 = the longest time ago.

a There was a meeting yesterday.
b He was at Ras Tanura from 2000 to 2008.
c We're busy.
d There was a big problem this morning.
e The cable trays were ready last Friday.
f I was in Dubai last month.
g He was in Ecuador last year.
h Consumption was one trillion m³ in 1970.

4 Answer the questions.

Useful expressions

last Monday	last month	in 2000
last week	this morning	yesterday

1 When were you busy?
2 When was your last holiday?
3 When were you ten years old?
4 When were you at a restaurant?
5 When was your last exam?

5 Work in pairs. Talk about the past. Ask and answer the questions in **4**.

earthquake (n) violent shaking of the ground

reserves (n) gas and oil in the ground

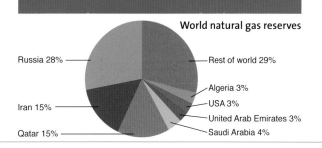

World natural gas reserves

Russia 28% — Rest of world 29%

Algeria 3%

USA 3%

United Arab Emirates 3%

Iran 15% — Saudi Arabia 4%

Qatar 15% —

Reading

The Sakhalin II Project

1 Answer the questions.

1 Do you know about the Sakhalin II project?
2 Look at the pictures. What places and things can you see?
3 What can you say or guess about the project?

2 Read the text. Answer the questions.

1 How many other LNG plants are in Russia?
2 How much gas comes from Sakhalin II?
3 Where is the liquefaction plant?
4 How much was in the first shipment to Japan?
5 What materials are in the two LNG tanks?
6 What environmental danger is mentioned?

3 Look at the map. Answer the questions.

1 Where are the producing regions?
2 Where is the shipping facility?
3 On the ship, what areas does the LNG go through?
4 Where is the LNG vaporized?
5 On the map, what is the name of the consuming region?

4 Guess the meaning of the words in **bold**. Use your dictionary if necessary.

1 What is the **capacity** of each holding tank?
2 What is the **lifespan** of the project?
3 What is the **quantity** of reserves?

5 Answer the questions in **4**.

6 Are there LNG facilities in your country? What are they? Where are they?

The Sakhalin II Project

The Sakhalin II project takes gas and oil from the Piltun-Astokhoskoye and Lunskoye fields. It's Russia's first liquefied natural gas plant and one of the biggest oil and gas developments in the world. Production is about 9.6 million tonnes of natural gas per year. The two fields probably contain 500 billion m^3 of natural gas **reserves**.

There are two 100,000 m^3 LNG tanks at Prigorodnoye. Each tank has an inner tank and an outer tank. The inner tank is steel, and the outer tank is concrete. The tanks' storage temperature is -165 °C. The tanks should be safe even in a big **earthquake**.

Sakhalin II supplies about 8% of global LNG. Work will continue there for 30–40 years.

Pipes carry the gas from the fields to the natural gas liquefaction facilities in Prigorodnoye, Sakhalin. Tankers take the LNG from the terminal at Prigorodnoye to Japan and other East Asian consumers.

Sakhalin's first gas shipment to Japan was in April, 2009. It was 145,000 m^3. The receiving terminal was in Sodegaura, near Tokyo.

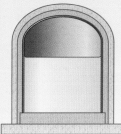

Piltun-Astokhskoye (oil and gas field)

Lunskoye (gas field)

Onshore pipeline (gas and oil)

SAKHALIN ISLAND

Prigorodnoye (LNG/oil shipping facility)

Sea of Japan

Pacific Ocean

JAPAN

TOKYO

Sodegaura (vaporization)

rot (v) to decay, or make sth decay, naturally and gradually

Speaking

Describing equipment

1 Match the shape with the name.

1 a cylinder   2 a sphere   3 a cube

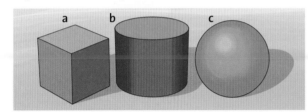

2 🎧 Listen and check your answers.

3 Match each description with a picture.

1 It's above-ground. __f__   6 It's on a truck. _____

2 It's cuboid. _____   7 It's spherical. _____

3 It's cylindrical. _____   8 It's underground. _____

4 It's horizontal. _____   9 It's vertical. _____

5 It's at a 90° angle. _____

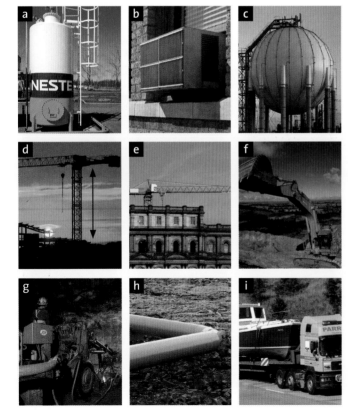

4 🎧 Listen and check your answers.

5 Practise describing equipment. Student A, go to p.109. Student B, go to p.113.

Practise describing equipment. Student A, go to p.109. Student B, go to p.113.

USEFUL LANGUAGE

Shape	Orientation	Location
cylindrical	vertical	on a tanker
spherical	horizontal	on wheels
cuboid		above-ground
		underground

It's my job

1 What do you know about biogas?

2 Look at the picture of the biogas plant. Describe the equipment.

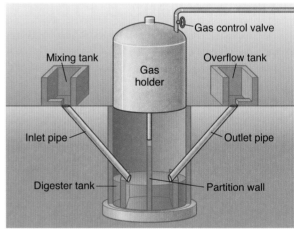

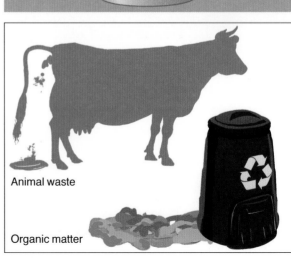

Checklist

Assess your progress in this unit. Tick (✓) the statements which are true.

- [ ] I can talk about gas production and distribution
- [ ] I can talk about a bar chart
- [ ] I can use Past Simple *be*
- [ ] I can understand the difference between past and present
- [ ] I can describe equipment

3 Read. Write T (true) or F (false).

1 Biogas comes from underground reserves.
2 Biogas is mostly methane.
3 Electricity and gas are easy to get in Rwanda.
4 A lot of Rwandans are farmers.
5 Rwanda is planning 300 biogas plants.

Jean-Claude Hakizimana

Biogas can come from organic matter, for example rotting plants and animal waste. When these things rot and there is no oxygen, they make methane.

I live in Rwanda, near the centre of Africa. We're a very poor country. Most people here have no electricity and no gas. But we are improving our country. Most people here live by farming. Most people in the countryside have cows, so in fact, we have plenty of animal waste.

We are making small biogas plants. They can make gas from animal waste. The dung from two or three cows is enough to make gas for cooking and lighting for one house. We now have more than 300 biogas plants around the country, and we're building more.

I am happy making life better here. And we are doing this with waste. Amazing.

4 Can biogas work easily in your country? Why / why not?

Project

Biogas is a source of energy that doesn't come from petroleum. Find out about others.

Key words

Adjectives
above-ground
cuboid
cylindrical
horizontal
liquid
spherical
underground
vertical

Nouns
ammonia
liquefied natural gas (LNG)
methane
vapour

Verbs
consume
liquefy
vaporize

Look back through this unit. Find five more words or expressions that you think are useful.

10 Oil and the environment

Kick off

1 Look at these pictures. Which shows
   1 an oil spill?   2 noisy equipment?   3 broken equipment?   4 a gas flare?

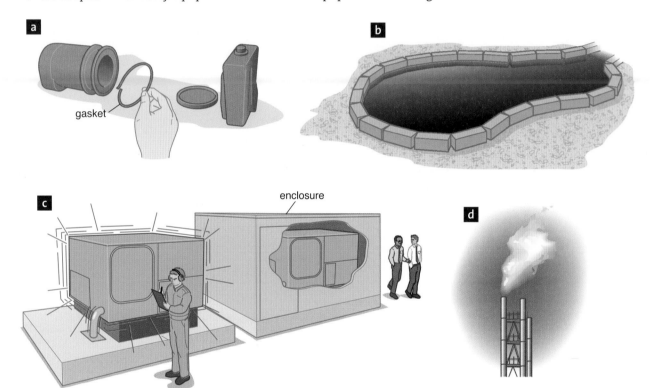

2 Which of the above can lead to
   1 noise pollution? *a, c, d*   2 water pollution?   3 soil pollution?   4 air pollution?

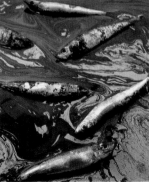

3 Match each solution below with a picture in 1.
   1 Reduce the noise.   2 Make it safe. Clean it up.   3 Repair it.   4 Limit or stop it.

● Language spot

Past Simple

We use the Past Simple to talk about the past.

Positive: *We started cleaning up last night.*

Negative: *We didn't start cleaning up last night.*

Question: *Did you start cleaning up last night?*

≫ Go to **Grammar reference** p.122

1 Complete each sentence with a word from the list. Use the Past Simple.

arrive   burn   go   have   start

EXAMPLE

We started cleaning up last night.

1 The crew _____ at 6.30.

2 The refinery fire _____ for three days.

3 I _____ to college in Abu Dhabi.

4 When we opened the flow, we _____ a lot of problems with the new pipeline.

do   make   see   start   stop

EXAMPLE

Did you start cleaning up last night?

5 Did we _____ a phone call to head office this morning?

6 Did they _____ work at three o'clock yesterday because of the bad weather?

7 Did you _____ a training course in the UAE last summer?

8 Did he _____ Khaled and Sami yesterday?

2 Make sentences 1–4 in **1** negative.

EXAMPLE

We started cleaning up last night. →
We didn't start cleaning up last night.

1 _____

2 _____

3 _____

4 _____

3 Make questions. Use the Past Simple.

1 you / about / Did / the / learn / oil / at / industry / school / ?

2 industry / Why / you / did / choose / oil / the / ?

3 tools / school / Did / use / you / power / at / ?

4 you / How / learn / did / oil / about / jobs / ?

5 did / lessons / When / you / English / begin / ?

4 Work in pairs. Ask and answer the questions.

It's my job

1 Match the definitions with the words.

1 companies that do jobs for other companies

2 in a way that isn't dangerous

3 report about possible dangers

4 places where buildings, wells, refineries, etc. are built

a risk assessment

b safely

c construction sites

d contractors

2 Can you explain what a safety and environment officer does?

3 🎧 Listen. Number the words a–d in **1** in the order you hear them.

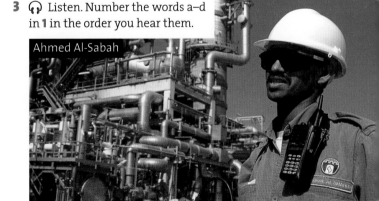

Ahmed Al-Sabah

4 🎧 Listen again. Answer the questions.

1 What company does Ahmed work for?

2 What does he help contractors do?

3 What did he work on last week?

4 What did he visit?

5 Who did he talk to?

6 What did he explain?

5 Would you like Ahmed's job? Why / why not?

prevent (v) to stop sb from doing sth; to stop sth from happening

procedure (n) a way of doing sth, especially the usual or correct way

protection programme (n) a plan to work in a way that keeps animals and the environment safe

technique (n) a particular way of doing sth, especially one in which you have to learn special skills

Vocabulary

Preventing and dealing with eco-hazards and incidents

- An eco-hazard is something that can harm the environment: people, plants, animals, water, earth, air.
- An incident is something that happens, an event: a fire, a gas leak, an oil spill, a collision, an accident.

1 Match sentences 1–6 with pictures a–f.

1 The fire started early this morning.
2 After the rig explosion, we improved our equipment and safety **procedures**.
3 We followed the usual procedure. We reported the spill immediately.
4 There was a gas leak. We wore hazmat suits when we checked the damage.
5 The field is under a beautiful beach, so we used special drilling **techniques**.
6 Our company has a wildlife **protection programme**. We studied the grey whales before we started drilling.

2 Complete the sentences with words from **1**.

Incidents

1 There was a f_____ . We put it out quickly.
2 There was an e_____ . It destroyed the rig.
3 There was an o_____ s_____ . We lost 10,000 litres.
4 There was a g_____ l_____ . We closed the main valve and made the area safe.

Preventing incidents

5 There are whales in the area, so we have a w_____ p_____ p_____ .
6 We follow s_____ p_____ . It's the best way to prevent accidents.
7 We use s_____ d_____ t_____ . We can get oil and protect nature.

3 Check your answers with a partner.

a

b

c

d

e

f

challenge (n) a new or difficult task that tests sb's ability and skill

nature reserve (n) an area where plants and animals are protected

On 20 April 2010, the drilling rig Deepwater Horizon exploded in the Gulf of Mexico. This caused an oil leak and a huge environmental disaster. The accident could have been prevented.

Reading

Preventing environmental damage

1 What environmental problems can oil drilling cause?

2 Look at the picture. What do you think it shows?

3 Read the text. Answer the questions.

1 What can you see in the area around Wytch Farm?
2 How many years passed between discovery and drilling?
3 What special drilling technique did British Gas use?
4 How far did some of the drilling go?

4 Find twelve Past Simple verbs in the text. Circle them.
Note: the Past Simple of *can't see* is *couldn't see*.

Wytch Farm

In 1973, the British Gas Corporation discovered a large oilfield in the south of England. There were 65 million tonnes of crude oil in the ground. And on the ground? A **nature reserve** including forests, trees, animals, birds, and a perfect beach and seaside – and a village. The engineers faced many **challenges**:

■ noise from construction and drilling
■ noise from trucks going to and from the site
■ bad smells from the site
■ possible oil spills, fires, and explosions
■ possible damage to the plants and animals in the area.

British Gas planned the work very carefully. They studied the plants and animals in the area and developed a wildlife protection programme. In 1979, they began drilling. They put the drilling rig in a wood. It was behind the trees so people couldn't see it easily. And they used a special drilling technique: horizontal drilling.

The easiest way to drill oil is straight down vertically into the oil. Horizontal drilling (sometimes called extended reach drilling) starts straight down, but then it turns. The drill goes into the oil from the side. Oil companies sometimes drill this way to help the oil flow into the well more

easily. But at Wytch Hill, it was a way to protect the environment. When you use horizontal drilling, the oil can be under a beautiful forest, a village, or even the sea, but the drilling rig and the gathering station can be far away. At Wytch Farm, some of the drilling started more than ten kilometres away from the oil.

Wytch Farm is the largest onshore oilfield in Western Europe. But environmental damage at the site is very small.

Br E	Am E
wood	forest

injury (n) harm done to a person's or animal's body

bund (Br E) = berm (Am E)

Contained

Uncontained

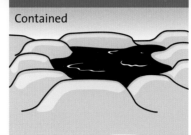 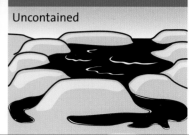

Listening

Problems and solutions

1 What can you see in the picture?

2 🎧 Listen to the conversations. Match each conversation with a problem.

Conversation	Problem
1 _____	a a leak
2 _____	b an oil spill
3 _____	c a noisy compressor

3 Choose the correct word in each sentence.

1 a *It's happen / It happened* last night.
   b We *closed / close* the main valve.

2 a Did it *work / worked*?
   b It *work / worked* very well.

3 a *It's started / It started* two days ago.
   b I *wait / waited* all day yesterday.

4 🎧 Listen and check your answers.

Pronunciation

1 🎧 Listen. Tick (✓) the sound of the *-ed* ending.

	verb+id	verb+t	verb+d
1 happened	☐	☐	☐
2 closed	☐	☐	☐
3 finished	☐	☐	☐
4 worked	☐	☐	☐
5 started	☐	☐	☐
6 waited	☐	☐	☐

2 🎧 Listen again. Check your answers.

3 Work in pairs. Read aloud the three conversations for *Listening* on p.129.

Speaking

Reporting an incident

1 🎧 Listen. Write T (true) or F (false).

1 There's an oil spill.   _____
2 It's between tanks 10 and 12. _____
3 There are no injuries.   _____
4 About 200 litres of oil spilled. _____
5 The spill is not contained.   _____

2 Work in pairs. Role-play reporting an incident. Student A, go to p.109. Student B, go to p.114.

Writing

An environmental incident report

Complete the report form. Use the words in the list.

no immediate risk   27 March   20,000 litres
Fazwan Area, Pipeline 32, Station 6   16.30
no damage after clean up   sand   pipeline leak

Environmental Incident Report

Date of incident: _____ 1

Time reported: _____ 2

Location: _____ 3

Type of incident: _____ 4

Volume of oil: _____ 5

Damage to: plants / wildlife / water / soil /

_____ 6

Risk assessment: _____ 7

Possible environmental damage:

_____
_____ 8

Project

Horizontal drilling protects the environment. Learn about other ways the oil industry protects the environment.

- double-hulled tankers
- re-planting after drilling
- safe disposal of drilling mud

Key words

Adjectives
dangerous
environmental
noisy

Adverbs
carefully
safely

Nouns
contractor
danger
eco-hazard
enclosure
explosion
incident
noise
risk assessment

Verbs
clean up
repair

Look back through this unit. Find five more words or expressions that you think are useful.

11 Workshop operations

Kick off

1 Look at these two workshops. Which one is

   1 neat and tidy?   2 messy?   3 safer?

2 In which workshop is it

   1 easy to lose tools?
   2 easy to find tools?
   3 easy to work?

3 Read the workshop rules. For each rule, find an example in picture a where the rule has been broken.

Workshop Rules

- Keep the floors tidy and dry.
- Keep the workbenches clean.
- Put tools away when you've finished a job.
- Don't block the exit.
- When you leave, turn off the lights and all of your equipment.

4 Is your room at home tidy or messy?

Listening

Workshop responsibilities

1 Match each workshop responsibility with an explanation.

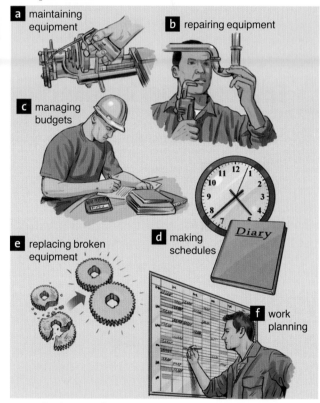

a maintaining equipment
b repairing equipment
c managing budgets
d making schedules
e replacing broken equipment
f work planning

   1 dealing with money
   2 organizing times and dates
   3 making broken things work
   4 taking care of machines, for example oiling them
   5 organizing people, equipment, and jobs
   6 taking out damaged parts and putting in new parts

2 🎧 Listen. Which responsibility (a–f above) are they talking about in each conversation?

   1 _____   3 _____   5 _____
   2 _____   4 _____   6 _____

3 🎧 Listen again. Check your answers.

4 Work in pairs.

   1 Name something that you have repaired.
   2 Name something that you have replaced.
   3 Name something that you maintain.

In this unit
- workshop rules and responsibilities
- managing the workshop
- power tools and their functions
- saying what's been done
- precision measurements
- writing a job card

Reading

Managing the workshop

1 What are smart ways to manage a workshop?

2 Read the text and see if your ideas were mentioned.

3 Find words in the text that mean
1 able to do a lot of work
2 an area where only one person may work
3 part of a tool that protects workers' fingers, hands, eyes, etc.
4 a danger or risk.

4 Match the opposites.

1	organized	a	dirty
2	clean	b	disorganized
3	clear (instructions)	c	cluttered
4	clear (workbench)	d	unsafe
5	safe	e	unclear

5 Choose three words from **4**. Write one example sentence for each word. Talk about something you know.

EXAMPLE
My desk at home is very cluttered.

6 Tell a partner.

Smart workshop management

A workshop manager's day is filled with problems: broken equipment in difficult locations; expensive repairs on small budgets; people working closely together using powerful tools and equipment. There will always be problems, but smart workshop management can make work easier, quicker, and safer.

Ten top tips

- Keep the workbenches clean and clear. A clean workshop is safer. It makes workers more productive.
- Keep the floors clean and dry.
- Create safety zones around large tools. The person who is using the tool can be inside the line. Others must stay outside the line.
- Use good lighting over work areas.
- Always put tools away after using them.
- Use guards on tools. Be sure that workers have and use personal protection equipment (PPE).
- Give clear work instructions for working safely. Tell workers what to do and how to do it.
- Take care of your workers. Maintain all machinery and tools. Stop using unsafe machines or tools.
- Spend time with your workers. Learn how they work. Everyone works differently. You may get some good ideas by watching.
- Watch for possible hazards. Use equipment and materials that can keep your workers safe.

A clean, organized workshop prevents problems.

Vocabulary

Power tools and their functions

1 Match each function with a picture.

1 grinding
2 cutting
3 welding
4 designing
5 turning and shaping
6 drilling

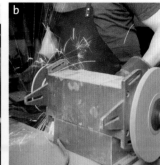

2 Work in pairs. Can you match each function above with a power tool or tools in the workshop picture below?

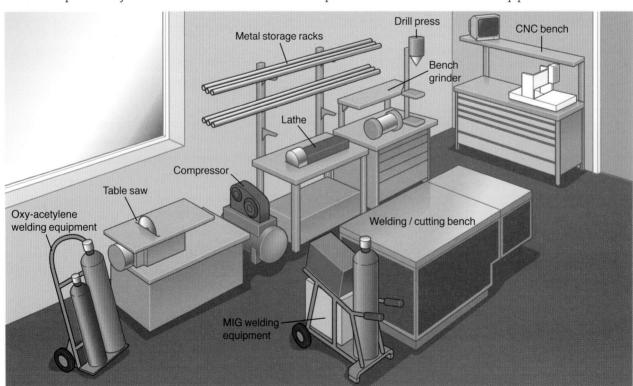

Measure twice, cut once.

Old saying

3 Complete the table.

Tool	Function
oxyacetylene equipment	welding and cutting metal
t_____¹ saw	cutting wood and metal
lathe	t_____² and shaping metal
storage rack	s_____³ pieces of metal
bench g_____⁴	grinding
drill press	d_____⁵
CNC bench	d_____⁶ and making metal parts
cutting and welding b_____⁷	working on cutting and welding jobs
MIG equipment	w_____⁸

4 Check your answers with a partner.

5 Unscramble the names of the portable power tools.

1 redgirn _____

2 lilrd _____

3 was _____

6 Work in pairs. Take turns asking and answering questions.

EXAMPLE

A *What do you do with oxyacetylene equipment?*

B *We weld and cut metal.*

● **Language spot**

Present Perfect

We use the Present Perfect

● to talk about recent actions.

A *Have you finished the work on the compressor?*

B *We've replaced the gaskets, but we haven't put the new bearings in.*

A *Has Ahmed phoned?*

B *No, he hasn't.*

● to talk about our lives.

A *Have you ever used a drill press?*

B *No, I've never used a drill press. Have you?*

A *Yes, I have.*

>> Go to Grammar reference p.122

1 Use the cues. Make Present Perfect sentences.

1 you finish welding ?

_____

2 we do the grinding

_____

3 you and Ahmed paint it?

_____

4 we not paint it

_____

5 they build the base?

_____

6 they not finish base

_____

7 they check the inside?

_____

8 Simon check inside

_____

9 they not repair the valve

_____

2 Tell a partner. Do you have any experience with the tools in *Vocabulary*? Which tools have you used?

EXAMPLE

A *Have you ever used a drill press?*

B *No, I've never used a drill press. Have you?*

A *Yes, I have.*

tolerance (n) the amount by which the measurement of a value can vary without causing problems

Mosquito

Speaking
Saying what's been done

Work in pairs. Student A, go to p.110. Student B, read the information below.

1 You are responsible for building an oil tank containment. You will build it in the workshop area then deliver it by truck to the site. Your manager telephones and asks you some questions. Look at the pictures. Answer the questions in full sentences. Use the Present Perfect. It is Tuesday.

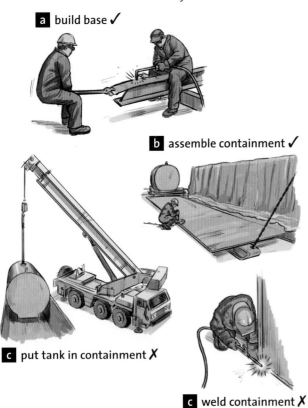

a build base ✓

b assemble containment ✓

c put tank in containment ✗

c weld containment ✗

2 Now it is Wednesday. You have left another worker (Student A) in charge of the containment project. Call them. Ask questions using the Present Perfect.

1 do grinding?
2 checked inside the tank?
3 attached the cover?
4 put the tank on the truck?

3 Now tell Student A three things you have done today and three things you haven't done today.

Number talk
Precision measurements

1 How do you say it? Read the words aloud.

1 mm	one millimetre
2 mm	two millimetres
1 µm	one micron
2 µm	two microns
0.001 mm	point oh oh one millimetres
0.025 mm	point oh two five millimetres
±	plus or minus

2 🎧 Listen and check your answers.

3 Read the information. Answer the questions.

> - 1 mm = 1,000 µm
> - 1 µm = 0.001 mm
> - A CNC milling machine has a tolerance of ± 25 µm.
> - The width of a human hair is 100 µm.
> - The diameter of a pinhead is 1 mm.
> - The length of a normal mosquito is 10 mm.

1 What is one hundred microns?
2 What is plus or minus twenty-five microns?
3 What is one millimetre?
4 What is about one centimetre?
5 How much is one micron in millimetres?
6 How much is one millimetre in microns?

4 Match the pictures with the measurements.

3–8 µm   5 mm   100 µm   10 mm

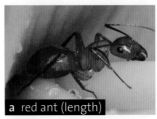
a red ant (length)

b spider's web (diameter)

c paint (thickness)

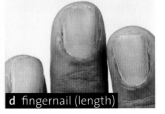
d fingernail (length)

Checklist

Assess your progress in this unit. Tick (✓) the statements which are true.

- [ ] I can talk about workshop rules and responsibilities
- [ ] I can talk about workshop management
- [ ] I can understand tools and their functions
- [ ] I can say what's been done
- [ ] I can talk about precision measurements
- [ ] I can write a job card

Writing

A job card

1 Read the note. Answer the questions.

1 What's the problem?
2 What has Roger asked Simon to do?
3 How long will the job probably take?

> Simon,
> The discharge hose in the bulk tanker loading area, bay 3, is leaky. Could you check it, please? Take a spare valve with you. Go over there at 8.00 tomorrow (Wednesday 12 April) morning. You should finish by 11.00. I've already done the paperwork (risk assessment, permit to work).
> Thanks,
> Roger

2 Use the information from the note. Complete the job card.

JOB CARD

Job card number: 2727505B
Area location: Bulk tanker _____¹, bay 3
Tasks: Check _____² valve on discharge hose
Materials required: Spare _____ ³
Scheduled start (date, time): _____ ⁴
Scheduled finish (date, time): _____ ⁵
Risk assessment: ☐ yes ☐ no⁶
Permit to work required: ☐ yes ☐ no⁷

Approval
Signature: *Roger Briggs*
Date: 11 April 20—
Assigned to: Simon Meeks

3 Now it's 8.10 on Wednesday. Answer the questions.

1 Has Roger done the risk assessment?
2 Has Simon started the job?
3 Has Simon finished the job?

Key words

Adjectives
broken
cluttered
messy
precision
tidy

Nouns
budget
containment
micron
responsibility
schedule
workbench

Verbs
maintain
manage
organize
replace

Look back through this unit. Find five more words or expressions that you think are useful.

12 Repairs and maintenance

Kick off

Work in pairs. Match the sentences with the pictures.

a We repaired the hose.
b The pump stopped working.

c We installed the pump.
d We reinstalled the pump.

e We replaced the bearing.
f We removed the pump.

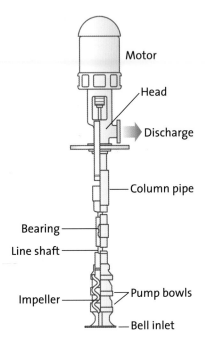

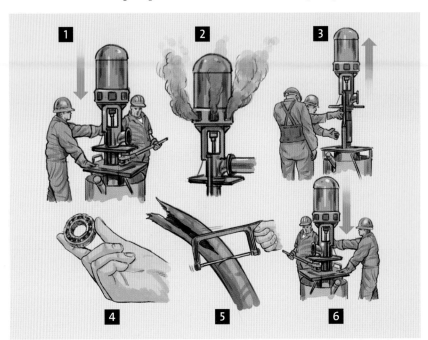

Vocabulary

Problems and solutions

1 🎧 Listen to the conversation. Choose the correct word.

1 The bearing was *frozen / broken*.

2 The bearing *was / wasn't* replaced.

3 The hose *was / wasn't* replaced.

4 The hose was *split / bent*.

frozen (can't move)

broken

split

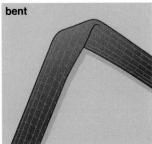

bent

2 🎧 Listen again and check your answers.

3 Look at the pictures in *Kick off*. The conversation happens after which picture?

4 Look at the pictures. Find the things.

1 a belt	4 a copier	7 a tank
2 a bolt	5 a gear	8 a wire
3 a computer	6 a cap	

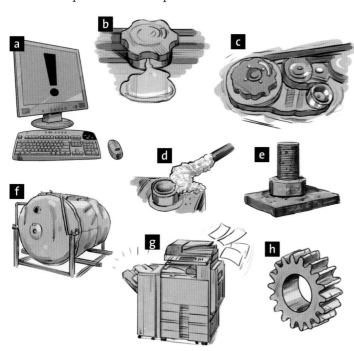

5 Match the sentence halves to describe the pictures.

1	The wires	a	is worn.
2	The tank	b	are corroded.
3	The computer	c	is jammed.
4	The copier	d	is leaking.
5	The bolt	e	is loose. So it's noisy.
6	The gear	f	is rusted.
7	The belt	g	is frozen. The system is down.
8	The cap	h	is damaged. There's a big dent in it.

6 🎧 Listen and check your answers.

7 🎧 Listen again. Which problem does each solution match?

a I'll check it.
b I'll clean them.
c I'll get the angle grinder.
d I'll get the manual.
e I'll re-start the system.
f I'll tighten it.
g I'll write a report.
h I'll replace it.

• Language spot

will

- We use *will* when we decide what to do.

A *It's leaking.*
B *I'll check it.*

- We use *will* when we talk about the future.

A *When **will** you finish?*
B *We **won't** finish before midnight.*

>> Go to **Grammar reference** p.123

1 Complete the short conversations. Use the words in the list in each conversation.

will   'll   won't

A The belt is broken.
B I _____[1] replace it.
A _____[2] you finish the job today?
B No, I _____[3].

A _____[4] Khalid be here tomorrow?
B No, he _____[5]. He _____[6] be here on Tuesday.

A The gasket's damaged.
B We _____[7] replace it.

A _____[8] we have time tomorrow?
B No, we _____[9].

2 Say what you will do in each situation. Use *will*.

EXAMPLE
'The belt's worn out.' → *I'll replace it.*

1 'I need the angle grinder.'
2 'I can't lift this box.'
3 'I can't find my goggles.'
4 'I don't have time to write the repair report.'
5 'The batteries need to be replaced.'

3 Work in pairs. Talk about your things that need repair and maintenance.

EXAMPLES
Tomorrow, I'll change the oil in my car.
Next year, I'll paint my bedroom.

USEFUL LANGUAGE

Tomorrow ... Next week ... Next month ...

Next year ... In two years ...

portable electric generator (n) a petrol-powered machine that makes electricity, used to power lights and tools on sites with no other electrical supply

Pronunciation

1 🎧 Listen. Which sentence do you hear?

1 a Turn the cab.   b Turn the cap.
2 a Repair the RIB.   b Repair the rip.
3 a Pull the tab.   b Pull the tap.

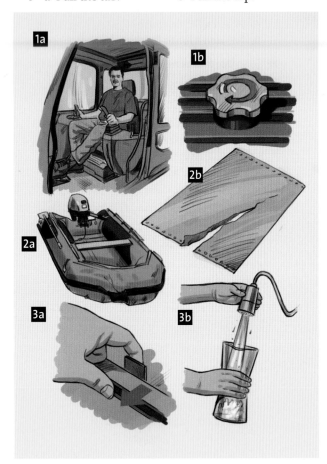

2 🎧 Compare answers with a partner. Then listen again and check your answers.

3 Complete these words from *Vocabulary*. Write *p* or *b*.

1 ____elt   5 ca____
2 ____olt   6 ____roken
3 com____uter   7 re____air
4 co____ier   8 ____roblem

4 🎧 Listen and repeat. Check your answers.

5 Work in pairs. Practise saying the sentences in **1**. Can your partner tell which sentence you're saying?

Reading

Routine maintenance

1 Do you own a machine that needs routine maintenance? What is the machine? What maintenance does it need? Tell a partner.

Portable Electric Generator

Routine maintenance is important for the generator's safe operation and long life. Routine maintenance is especially important in hot and dusty environments. The schedule at the right shows the procedures and frequency for basic maintenance. The generator's hour meter shows the number of hours that the generator has run.

2 Read the paragraph above. For each word or phrase below, write T (time) or A (action).

1 routine maintenance _____
2 long life   _____
3 procedure   _____
4 number of hours   _____

3 Tick (✔) the ideas that the text mentions about maintenance.

1 It can reduce accidents and injuries.   ☐
2 It can save time and money.   ☐
3 It can help a machine work well for many years. ☐
4 Heat and dust can damage a machine.   ☐

4 Look at the maintenance schedule below. Which statement isn't correct?

1 A month has passed. The hour meter says 15 hours have passed. I'll clean and check the battery.
2 Six months have passed. The hour meter says that 200 hours have passed. I'll replace the air filter.
3 Eleven months have passed. The hour meter says 250 hours have passed. I'll wait one more month and then change the spark plug.

MAINTENANCE PROCEDURE	MAINTENANCE FREQUENCY			
	Every day or 8 hours	1 month or 20 hours	9 months or 200 hours	12 months or 300 hours
General inspection	✗			
Check engine oil level	✗			
Clean and check battery		✗		
Change engine oil			✗	
Replace air filter			✗	
Replace spark plug				✗
Replace fuel filter				✗

5 Look at the maintenance record below. Answer the questions.

1 Has this generator been well maintained?
2 Say what they haven't done.

EXAMPLE

They haven't inspected the generator every day.

DATE	HOUR METER READING	MAINTENANCE OR SERVICE PERFORMED
20/1/20–	20	general inspection, checked engine oil level – OK
25/3/20–	85	general inspection, cleaned and checked battery
15/5/20–	89	changed air filter
19/7/20–	265	general inspection, changed engine oil, cleaned and checked battery
20/7/20–	1	2
21/7/20–	281	3
22/7/20–	285	4
23/7/20–	289	5

6 Now look at the maintenance schedule. Fill in the gaps showing correct routine maintenance.

give (someone) a hand (v) help (someone)

Spark

Electrocution

Listening

Planning the day's work

1 Which job would a mechanic probably do? Write M. Which job would an electrician probably do? Write E.

1 check a photocopier
2 check the petrol engine of a portable generator

2 🎧 Listen to Frank planning the day's work with his team. Write the jobs.

Name	Jobs
Frank Workshop manager	morning _____ 1 afternoon _____ 2
Eric Office manager	morning _____ 3 afternoon _____ 4
Carl Electrician	morning _____ 5 afternoon _____ 6
Bill Mechanic	morning _____ 7 afternoon _____ 8

3 🎧 Listen again. Answer the questions.

1 How did the front office report their problem to Eric?
2 Carl may ask for help with the photocopier. Who will he ask?
3 Who has a problem with the generator?
4 When did Bill finish the repairs on the pump?
5 When did the new lights for the loading area arrive?

4 🎧 Listen again and check your answers to **2** and **3**.

It's my job

1 Work in pairs. Say the names of electrical things that you use every day.

2 Read the text. Which topics does Carlos talk about?

1 His education and training
2 His duties and responsibilities
3 The dangers of his work
4 The equipment he uses for troubleshooting
5 Safety on the job

Carlos Sanchez

I'm an electrician. I work on anything and everything electrical in the oil industry. I help to install, maintain, and repair electrical wiring, fixtures, and control equipment. This includes troubleshooting when things go wrong. A lot of my work is outdoors. I work in all kinds of weather. Sometimes I work in very high places. During any working week, I use all of my personal protective equipment (PPE): hard hat, safety glasses with side shields, safety shoes, safety gloves, hearing protection, fire retardant clothing, safety harness, and breathing apparatus. I also use a special insulating rubber matting. I can stand or sit on it when I work. It reduces the risk of shock.

Electricity creates two main hazards. The first is electrocution. If electricity enters your body, it can burn you badly or kill you. The other hazard is sparks. Sparks are generally hazardous, but especially in the oil and gas industry. If there is a spark in an area with flammable gas, of course there can be an explosion.

I work very carefully and check everything. Is the electricity switched off? Am I using the right PPE? And other electricians check my work too. We look out for each other.

3 Would you like to do Carlos's job? Why / why not?

Checklist

Assess your progress in this unit. Tick (✓) the statements which are true.

- [ ] I can talk about problems and solutions
- [ ] I can use *will* to talk about the future
- [ ] I can understand routine maintenance
- [ ] I can plan a day's work
- [ ] I can record repairs

Writing

Recording repairs

1 Read the repair record. Put the notes in the correct place.

Checked belt tension   Checked oil level
Compressor making strange noise
Loose belt   Tightened belt

REPAIR RECORD	Date: 9 April 20—
Item to repair: Portable air compressor	
Problem: _____	1
Troubleshooting notes	
_____	2
_____	3
Cause: _____	4
Repair: _____	5

2 Look at the pictures. Complete the repair record.

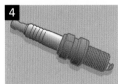

1 won't start
2 engine oil
3 spark plug
4 dirty
5 clean

REPAIR RECORD	Date: 9 April 20—
Item to repair: Portable generator	
Problem: _____	1
Troubleshooting notes	
_____	2
_____	3
Cause: _____	4
Repair: _____	5

3 Compare answers with a partner.

Key words

Nouns
belt
bolt
gear
maintenance
troubleshooting

Verbs
install
reinstall
remove

Adjectives
bent
corroded
damaged
frozen
jammed
rusted
split
worn

Look back through this unit. Find five more words or expressions that you think are useful.

13 The refinery

Kick off

1 Match the petroleum product with a picture.

asphalt / bitumen   liquid petroleum gas   petrol / gasoline   kerosene / jet fuel   diesel / petrodiesel   fuel oil

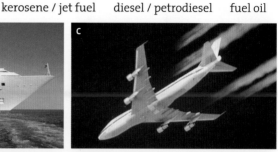

2 Can you name other ways each product is used?

3 Answer the questions.

1 Which product is the heaviest?
2 Which is the lightest?
3 Which is a solid?
4 Which ones are liquids?
5 Which burns as a gas?

Listening

A refinery tour

1 🎧 Listen to the presentation about Oakton refinery. Match each description (1–9) with a place (a–i) in the picture on p.89.

2 🎧 Listen again. Check your answers.

3 Complete the sentences. Use the words in the list.

bring   is connected   is hidden   is refined
is returned   is stored   manage   take   travels

1 This is the jetty. Tankers _____ crude oil to the refinery. They unload the crude oil here.

2 The crude oil _____ along these pipes into the tanks at the tank farm.

3 The crude oil _____ in these tanks until it is refined. Some of them are 80 metres high. There are over 200 steps to the top.

4 This is the main refinery. This is where the oil _____ in the distillation towers.

5 These pipes take the products out of the refinery. Some of the pipes _____ kerosene to the airport.

6 The refinery uses river water for cooling the machinery. The used water _____ here, to the salt marsh. It is often cleaner when it is returned than it was when it was taken from the river.

7 The refinery _____ to the main road here. All of the workers come and go this way. Some of our products leave this way in tankers.

8 The admin block is where the offices are. The people who work here _____ the people and all of the machinery at the refinery.

9 Oakton is the neighbouring village. The refinery _____ from the village by trees.

In this unit
● listening to a refinery tour
● using the Passive
● explaining a process
● talking about temperature
● reading about fractional distillation

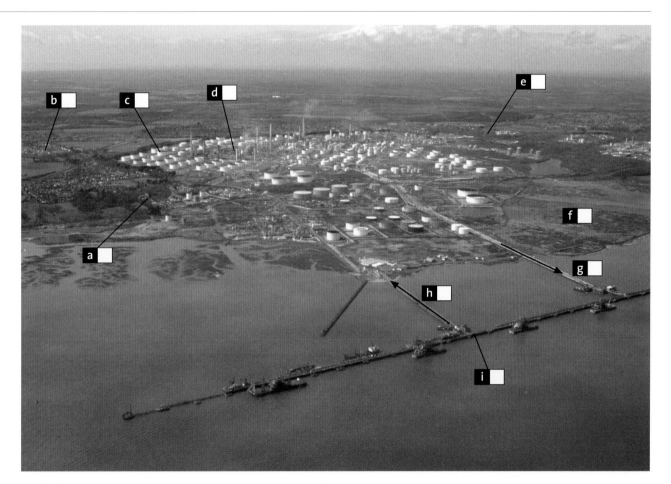

4 🎧 Listen again and check your answers.

5 Answer the questions.
1 Where is the crude oil stored?
2 Where is the crude oil refined?
3 Where is water returned to the river?
4 Where are products taken out of the refinery?

● Language spot

The Passive

● We use Passive verbs to explain actions or processes.
*The crude oil **is refined** in the refinery.*

● Sometimes you can choose to use the Active or the Passive.
*The pipes **take** the oil from the ships.* (Active)
*The oil **is taken** from the ships by the pipes.* (Passive)

>> Go to **Grammar reference** p.123

1 Choose the correct word.
1 The trees *hide / are hidden* the refinery.
2 The refinery *is managed / manages* from the admin block.
3 Some products *leave / are left* the refinery in tankers.
4 Kerosene *is taken / takes* to the airport by a pipeline.
5 The crude oil *is refined / refines* in the distillation towers.
6 Tankers *unload / are unloaded* their oil at the jetty.
7 The crude oil *stores / is stored* in the tanks.
8 The distillation towers *are distilled / distil* the crude oil.

2 Tick (✓) the sentences in **1** that are passive.

earth (v) (Br E) connect an electrical device with the ground.
Am E = *ground*

transport emergency card (n) a card with information about what a lorry driver should do in case of an emergency. It also includes information about the product that is carried.

3 Match the actions with the pictures.

a Check the transport emergency card.
b Connect the pipes.
c Drain the hoses.
d Load the tanker.

e Earth the tanker.
f Switch off the master switch.
g Drive the tanker into the loading area.
h Drive the tanker out of the loading area.

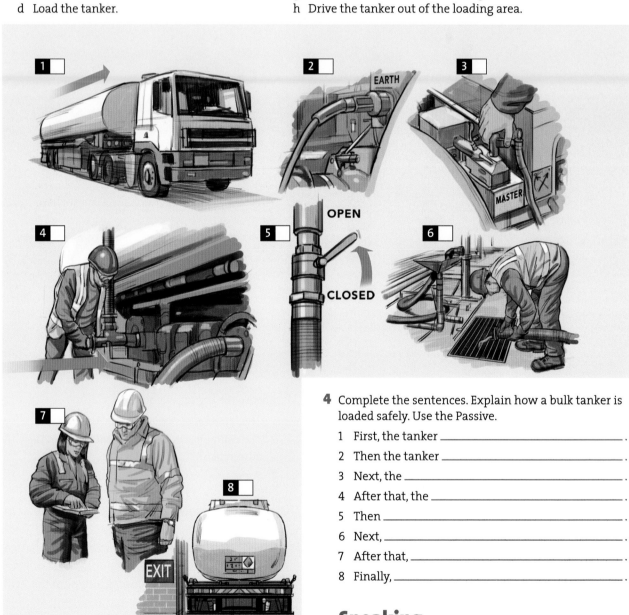

4 Complete the sentences. Explain how a bulk tanker is loaded safely. Use the Passive.

1 First, the tanker _____ .
2 Then the tanker _____ .
3 Next, the _____ .
4 After that, the _____ .
5 Then _____ .
6 Next, _____ .
7 After that, _____ .
8 Finally, _____ .

Speaking

Explaining a process

Work in pairs. Take turns describing a process. Student A, go to p. 110. Student B, go to p. 114.

monitor (v) to watch and check sth over a period of time in order to see how it develops, so that you can make any necessary changes

production (n) amount of a product that is made, for example 14.5 million litres of petrol per day

troubleshoot (v) find and correct problems in a mechanical, electrical, or electronic system

Number talk

Temperature

1 Match the numbers with the words.

1	-40 °C	a	minus forty degrees Celsius
2	0 °C	b	thirty-seven degrees Celsius
3	45 °C	c	zero degrees Celsius
4	37 °C	d	one hundred degrees Celsius
5	100 °C	e	forty-five degrees Celsius

2 🎧 Listen and check your answers.

3 Complete the sentences with the temperatures in **1**.

1 _____ °C is an average summer temperature in Saudi Arabia.

2 Ice melts at _____ °C.

3 Water boils at _____ °C.

4 Normal body temperature is _____ °C.

5 _____ °C is a cold winter day in Alaska.

4 Take the temperature quiz. Complete the sentences with the numbers in the list.

-42   200   250   400   600

1 In a refinery, crude oil is heated to about _____°C.

2 Asphalt usually boils at more than _____°C.

3 The boiling point of LP gas is usually about _____°C.

4 Petrol often boils at _____°C.

5 The boiling point of kerosene is usually about _____°C.

1 600 2 400 3 -42 4 200 5 250

It's my job

1 Can you guess what a process technician does?

1 monitors the refinery equipment ☐

2 organizes the schedule of crude oil delivery ☐

3 deals with environmental complaints ☐

4 takes care of troubleshooting and repairs ☐

5 tests the refinery's products ☐

2 Read and check your answers.

3 Answer the questions.

1 How many people work at Suparman's refinery?

2 What two reasons does he give for shutting down?

3 What maintenance job does he mention?

4 How much time do they take to plan a shut down?

5 What two refinery products does he mention?

Suparman Perkasa

I work at an oil refinery in Sumatra, Indonesia. It's a big refinery. There are more than 300 tanks and nearly 1,000 workers. My team takes care of all of the refinery equipment. When the refinery is running normally, we **monitor** all of the equipment. This means we check and maintain everything. When there is a problem, we **troubleshoot** it. That means trying to understand what's wrong. Then we try to repair it. We work closely with the maintenance team. Sometimes, we need to shut down part of the refinery for a big repair job and for some maintenance jobs, for example furnace cleaning. Shutting down means safely stopping some of the machines. But you can't just switch it off! We usually schedule a maintenance shut down a year in advance. We work closely with an experienced, specialist contractor. Another important job is checking the products that are made in the refinery. This means we test the petrol, the kerosene, and so on to make sure it is good. My team also writes in the **production** log. The production log is the information about how much crude oil we have processed and how much of each product we have made.

World's top three refineries in production		
Name of refinery	**Location**	**Litres per day**
Paraguana Refining Complex	Venezuela	149.5 million
SK Energy Ulsan Refinery	South Korea	133.5 million
Yeosu Refinery	South Korea	111.3 million

Br E	Am E
lorry	truck

Reading

Fractional distillation

1 Can you explain how an oil refinery works?

2 Read the text. Use the words in **bold** to label the picture (1–5).

How a refinery works

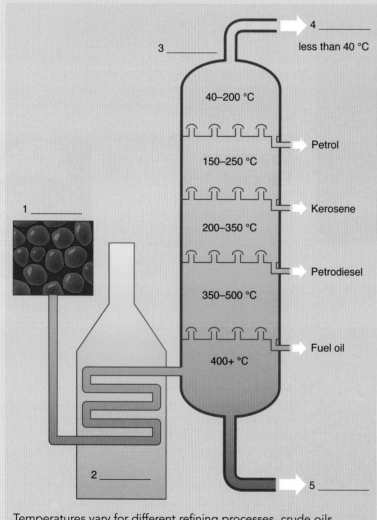

Temperatures vary for different refining processes, crude oils, and end products.

An oil refinery turns **crude oil** into **petroleum gas**, petrol / gasoline, kerosene, diesel oil, fuel oil, **asphalt / bitumen**, and many other products. Here's how it works. First, the crude oil is pumped into the **furnace**, where it is boiled. Next, the boiling oil enters the bottom of the **distillation tower**. Boiling separates the crude oil into fractions. *Fraction* means *part*. The fractions of crude oil are products with different boiling points: petroleum gas, petrol, and so on. The lightest product, petroleum gas, rises to the top. The heaviest products, like asphalt, sink to the bottom. After the products are separated, they are piped out of the tower. The different products are stored in tanks in the refinery. Finally, they are taken out of the refinery by tanker lorry, rail tanker, boat, or pipeline.

Refineries and the environment

In addition to making useful petroleum products, fractional distillation and other refinery processes also can create noise, odour, air pollution, and water pollution. Most countries have environmental rules that refineries must follow. All refineries must monitor and control possible problems. Every refinery has a safety and environment officer. His or her job is to make sure the refinery follows the rules.

3 Answer the questions.

1 Which product has a boiling point of about 350 °C?
2 Which is lighter, petrol or kerosene?
3 Which is the heaviest product on the picture?
4 What three vehicles does the text mention?
5 What environmental problems are mentioned?
6 Who has the job of monitoring possible environmental problems?

4 Work in pairs. Close your book. Draw a picture to explain fractional distillation. Write sentences to explain the process.

USEFUL LANGUAGE

First ...   Next ...   Then ...   After that ...   Finally ...

Writing
Explaining a process

1 Write a paragraph that explains a process.

- A paragraph is a group of sentences that explain an idea.

Look again at the process you explained in *Speaking* on p.90 (Student A role card p.110, Student B role card p.114). Write a paragraph that explains the process (loading a tanker train at a refinery or loading a bulk tanker at sea).

2 Compare your paragraphs with other students'. Did you say the same things?

Project

1 Find information on an oil refinery in your country.

- Where is it?
- How much oil does it process?
- How is crude oil delivered to the refinery?
- How are petroleum products taken away from the refinery?

2 Oil is sometimes measured in a 42-gallon barrel (about 159 litres). In a typical barrel of crude, how much will be refined into

- petroleum gas?
- petrol?
- kerosene?
- petrodiesel?
- fuel oil?
- asphalt?
- other products?

Key words

Nouns
asphalt
boil
bulk tanker
degrees Celsius (°C)
fractional distillation
fuel oil
furnace
gas
kerosene
liquid petroleum gas (LPG)
petrodiesel

Adjective
solid

Verbs
earth
melt
refine

Look back through this unit. Find five more words or expressions that you think are useful.

14 Emergencies

Kick off

1 Look at the pictures. Have you had an experience like this? What happened?

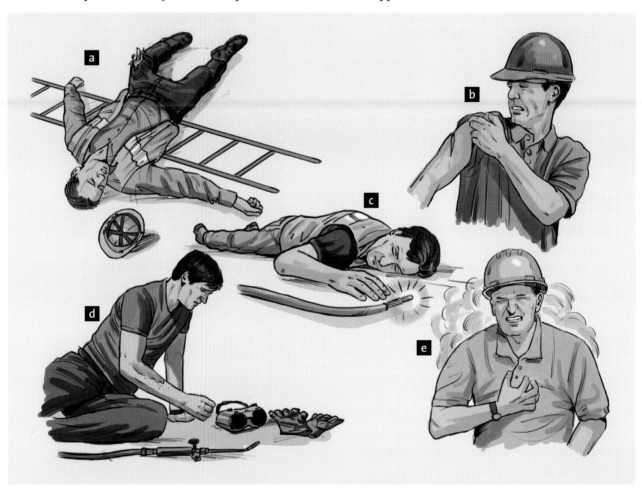

2 Match situations a–e above with descriptions 1–5.

1 He's having problems breathing. I think he breathed in some fumes.
2 He's cut his arm. He's bleeding.
3 He's broken his leg.
4 He's got a bad burn.
5 He's had an electric shock.

3 Match each piece of advice with a description (1–5) in **2**.

a Pour cold water on it and call emergency services. Keep it very clean!

b Stop his leg from moving. Call emergency services.

c Clean it. Then put a bandage on it.

d Make sure the electricity is off before you touch him.

e Gently move him to some fresh air. If you've got some oxygen, give it to him.

In this unit
- dealing with accidents and emergencies
- using *if / when / in case*
- emergency vehicles and equipment
- understanding what's wrong
- Past Continuous
- explaining and reporting accidents

Reading

Dealing with accidents and emergencies

1 If you see a situation like those in *Kick off*, what should you do?

2 Read and check your answers.

> **When there's an accident . . .**
>
> **1 Assess the situation.**
> - Try to understand what has happened. Do this quickly and calmly.
> - Check for danger. If something has injured somebody, will it also injure you?
> - Never do something that will injure you. If you do, then there may be two injured people.
>
> **2 Make the area safe.**
> - Protect the injured person from danger.
> - Be careful!
>
> **3 Assess the injured people and give emergency first aid.**
> - Assess each person.
> - Help the people with the worst injuries first.
> - Only treat an injured person if you are competent to do so.
>
> **4 Get help.**
> - Call emergency services or make sure that someone has called them.

3 Find words in the text for these definitions.

1 _____ (v) to judge and have an opinion about something

2 _____ (adv) in a quiet way, not excited or angry

3 _____ (v) to keep someone or something safe

4 Match each action with a section (1–4) of the text.

a I could see that he was burned, so I poured cold water on the burn.

b I saw him lying on the floor. Then I saw that there was a broken power cable.

c I used my mobile and phoned emergency services.

d I switched off the electricity so I wouldn't get shocked.

Br E	Am E
mobile	cell phone

5 Complete the text. Use the words in the list.

Activate   Call   Ensure   Remove   Try

> ## WHEN THERE'S A FIRE
>
> _____ [1] people from danger if you can do it safely.
>
> _____ [2] the doors are closed to stop the smoke and fire spreading.
>
> _____ [3] the fire alarm.
>
> _____ [4] emergency services.
>
> _____ [5] to put out the fire or help people leave the area.
>
> ## STAY CALM

6 Look at the first letter of each sentence. What word do they make?

_____ (v) to do something when something happens

It's my job

1 What do you usually do when you are sick or injured and need to see a doctor? What do you think workers on drilling rigs do?

Saresh Budhrani

2 🎧 Listen to Saresh Budhrani. Complete the sentences.

1 When someone is sick or injured, I _____ of them.

2 If someone is badly injured or very sick, I _____ evacuation.

3 When new employees arrive, I _____ them basic health and safety training.

4 If there's a fire, we _____ a fire-fighting plan.

5 We also have an evacuation plan, in case we need to _____ everyone off the rig quickly.

6 If there are problems with noise or waste management, for example, I _____ them.

3 🎧 Listen again and check your answers.

● Language spot

if / when / in case

- We use *if* and *when* to talk about expected situations.
  When someone is sick or injured, I take care of them.
  If someone is badly injured or very sick, I arrange evacuation.

- We use *in case* to talk about plans and preparations for possible emergencies.
  We also have an evacuation plan in case we need to get everyone off the rig quickly.

>> Go to **Grammar reference** p.124

1 Choose the correct words.

1 *When / In case* new employees start work, I train them.
2 We have a first aid kit *when / in case* someone gets hurt.
3 *If / In case* there's an accident, we need to complete a report.
4 *When / in case* the fire alarm rings, we stop work immediately and evacuate the building.
5 We always have a fire extinguisher nearby *if / in case* there's a fire and we need to use it quickly.
6 *If / In case* there's a problem, I try to deal with it quickly.

2 Complete the sentences using your own ideas.

1 When I'm sick or injured, I ...
2 If I have an English test, I ...
3 If the fire alarm rings, we ...
4 I try to save a little extra money in case ...
5 When the weather is very hot, I ...
6 I always carry my mobile phone in case ...

3 Make sentences to describe these signs. Use *if, when,* or *in case.*

EXAMPLE
When there's an electrical fire, don't use this fire extinguisher.

Vocabulary

Emergency vehicles and equipment

1 Can you name these things?

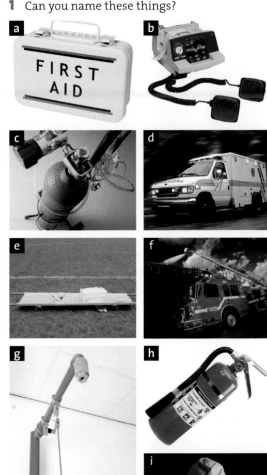

2 Match each name below with an item in **1**.

1	fire extinguisher	6	medical oxygen
2	first aid kit	7	emergency shower
3	ambulance	8	defibrillator
4	fire engine	9	SCBA (self-contained
5	stretcher		breathing apparatus)

3 Can you think of a situation where each item would be used?

conscious (adj) awake, alert, able to speak

unconscious (adj) not awake, usually because of an injury or illness

a minor injury (n) an injury that is not very serious

a serious injury (n) a bad or dangerous injury

---

4 For each situation 1–5, answer the questions. For ideas, look again at *Reading* on p.95.

  a What will you do?

  b Which emergency equipment will you use?

EXAMPLE

I'll check the area for danger. Then I'll try to help him. I'll use the first aid kit. I'll call emergency services.

1 A rigger has fallen from a high place. His leg is badly broken. The injury is serious. He is conscious but he is in a lot of pain.

2 A technician has cut his arm. It's a minor injury.

3 An electrician has had an electric shock. He's unconscious.

4 A welder has burned his arm.

5 There's a fire in the workshop. The workshop manager has just come out. He's having trouble breathing.

Listening

Understanding what's wrong

1 🎧 Listen to people talking in three emergencies. Write T (true) or F (false).

Situation 1

1 The man has broken his hand.

2 The injury is very serious.

3 The area is now safe.

Situation 2

4 The man has a serious head injury.

5 He's unconscious.

6 They telephone an ambulance.

Situation 3

7 The man was burned by a fire.

8 He used the emergency shower.

9 The injury is serious.

2 🎧 Listen again. Answer the questions.

Situation 1

1 Where was the incident?

2 What were the men doing?

3 What will they do now?

Situation 2

4 What fell on the man's head?

5 Can the injured man talk?

6 Where did the incident happen?

Situation 3

7 What part of the man's body was injured?

8 Where did the incident happen?

9 What do they need to do next?

3 🎧 Listen again. Check your answers.

● Language spot

Past Continuous

We use the Past Continuous to talk about continuing actions in the past. It is often used with the Past Simple.

Positive

*We **were welding** when the fire started.*

*I **was working** on the ladder this morning.*

Negative

*I **wasn't wearing** my goggles when I hurt my eye.*

*We **weren't using** the safety guard on the saw.*

Questions

***Were** you **welding** when the fire started?*

***Was** he **working** on the ladder this morning?*

1 Use the cues. Write sentences.

1 I (work) in Dubai last year.

2 We (not weld) yesterday when the fire started.

3 they (go) to the airport when the car broke down?

4 He (clean) the spark plugs.

5 You (not use) the hand guard.

6 she (use) her mobile phone when she was driving?

7 It (make) a strange noise so we turned it off.

8 I (not drive) the truck.

2 Answer the questions about yourself.

1 What were you doing last Monday morning?

2 What were you wearing yesterday?

3 Who were you talking to before English class?

4 What were you using the computer for last month?

5 When were you studying?

6 Where were you sitting in English class last time?

>> Go to **Grammar reference** p.124

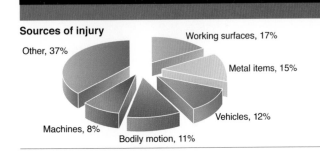

Sources of injury

Other, 37%
Working surfaces, 17%
Metal items, 15%
Vehicles, 12%
Bodily motion, 11%
Machines, 8%

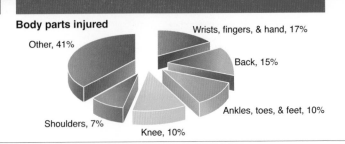

Body parts injured

Other, 41%
Wrists, fingers, & hand, 17%
Back, 15%
Ankles, toes, & feet, 10%
Knee, 10%
Shoulders, 7%

Pronunciation

1 Complete the words with *v* or *w*.

1 s____itch off   6 ____elding
2 ad____ice   7 ____ater
3 e____acuate   8 ____ery
4 acti____ate   9 ____orst
5 ____ehicle

2 🎧 Listen and check your answers.

3 🎧 Listen. Circle the word that you hear.

1 Do you know where it *vents / went*?
2 Did you get the *veal / wheel*?
3 We had a problem with a *wiper / viper*.

4 Work in pairs. Take turns reading the sentences above, saying either the first word or the second. Can your partner tell which word you're saying?

Speaking

Explaining an accident

1 Match the halves of the questions.

1 Where was   a the injuries?
2 What   b did it happen?
3 Who   c happened?
4 What are   d was there?
5 When   e the accident?

2 Read the report. Answer the questions in **1**.

Injury type: Broken leg

Work activity: Air conditioning repair

Location: Roof of admin block

Date and time of incident: 10.00 a.m. 8 July 20—

Description of incident:

John Green, Bill Becks, and Rolf Jordan were repairing the air conditioning in the admin block. Jordan was carrying a large piece of wood. He didn't see that a roof panel had been removed. He fell into the roof space and broke his leg.

3 Look at the pictures. Role-play this situation.

Student A, you saw the incident. Phone Student B, a medic, to report it.

Begin with *I need to report an accident.*

Student B, you are the medic. Answer Student A's phone call. Ask for details about the accident. Give advice.

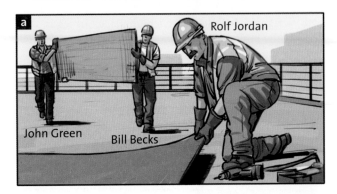

a   Rolf Jordan
John Green   Bill Becks

b

c

d

4 Do another role-play. Student A, go to p.111. Student B, go to p.115.

Checklist

Assess your progress in this unit. Tick (✓) the statements which are true.

- [ ] I can deal with accidents and emergencies
- [ ] I can understand what's wrong
- [ ] I can explain an accident
- [ ] I can write an accident report
- [ ] I can understand vital signs

Writing

An accident report

1 Complete an accident report.

1 Read the report in *Speaking* **2**.
2 Look again at the accident you explained in *Speaking* **4**.
3 Write a report about that accident.

Injury type: _____

Work activity: _____

Location: _____

Date and time of incident: _____

Description of incident: _____

_____

_____

2 Compare your answers with other students who wrote about the same accident.

Number talk

Vital signs

Vital signs are numbers that help medics understand a sick or injured person.

1 Look at the picture. Complete the text.

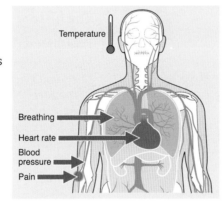

Temperature

Breathing

Heart rate

Blood pressure

Pain

- A fever is a _____[1] above 38.5 °C.
- A normal resting _____[2] rate is 60–100 beats per minute.
- A normal resting _____[3] rate is 12–20 breaths per minute.
- 85/55 is a low _____[4] pressure. 150/100 is high.
- _____[5] is measured on a scale of 1–10. 1 is very mild and 10 is the worst possible.

2 🎧 Listen and check your answers.

Key words

Nouns
ambulance
defibrillator
emergency shower
fire engine
fire extinguisher
first aid kit
medical oxygen
SCBA (self-contained breathing apparatus)
stretcher

Verbs
activate
assess
deal with
ensure
evacuate
react

Look back through this unit. Find five more words or expressions that you think are useful.

15 Petrochemicals

Kick off

1 Look at the pictures. Can you name these products?

2 Match the words with the pictures.

1 adhesives	4 plastics	7 rubber
2 fertilizer	5 carpeting	8 medications
3 paints	6 cosmetics	9 clothes

3 Petrochemicals are chemicals made from petroleum and petroleum gas. They are used to make all of the products in the pictures. Can you say what other materials can be used for some of the products? Think about plants, animals, and minerals (things from the ground, for example iron, sand, etc.).

Reading

The history of petrochemicals

1 Read the text *From carbon black to PVC*. Choose the correct definition for each word.

1 carbon black
   a a fuel   b a colouring
2 in prehistoric times
   a a very long time ago   b recently
3 plentiful
   a dangerous   b easy to find
4 inexpensive
   a cheap   b hard to get
5 crayon
   a a type of tyre   b a drawing tool
6 by-product
   a an extra, unneeded product
   b a flammable product
7 hydrocarbon molecule
   a petrochemicals
   b tiny pieces of hydrogen and carbon
8 familiar
   a known by many people   b useful
9 synthetic
   a man-made   b natural

2 Read the text again. Answer the questions.

1 What natural clothing materials does the text talk about?
2 What did the first big petrochemical plant make?
3 Why did the petrochemical business grow?
4 When were a lot of synthetic materials developed?
5 What synthetic cloth does the text mention?
6 Why are plastics sometimes a problem?

3 Name three things that you use every day that are made from petrochemical products.

4 Read the text about polymers. Write T (true) or F (false).

1 *Polymer* is another name for a single molecule.
2 Bakelite is a natural product.
3 Natural rubber is a polymer.

5 What products can you name that are made of the three polymers in the text?

Polymers

Nylon, polystyrene, and PVC are polymers. *Poly* means many, and *mer* means part. A polymer is many single molecules (called monomers) formed into a chain.

The first synthetic polymer – Bakelite – was first sold in 1909. It was used to make casings for radios and telephones, and also for kitchenware, jewellery, and toys.

Not all polymers are synthetic. Many natural products, for example rubber, are polymers.

From carbon black to PVC

Before oil and gas were freely available, people made everyday things from natural materials. Clothes were made from cotton, wool, and leather. Containers, for example bottles and cups, were made from metal, glass, and clay (soft earth that becomes hard when cooked). Paints and cosmetics were made from plants and minerals.

One example of a natural product is carbon black. It's a colouring used in ink for writing and drawing and for paint. It is made by burning wood, oil, or other natural materials. It was discovered in prehistoric times, and it's commonly used today.

The first petrochemical factory was built in 1872, and it made carbon black from natural gas. Carbon black wasn't a new product, but using a factory was a new way of making it. It became possible to make large amounts of it cheaply because natural gas was plentiful and inexpensive. At that time, carbon black was used to make ink, paint, and crayons. It is now used mostly to make car tyres.

In the early 1900s, the petrochemical business began to grow. There were a lot of oil refineries, and they created chemical by-products. Oil companies wanted to find ways to use these chemicals.

Soon scientists and engineers learned to change the hydrocarbon molecules in coal, petroleum, and refinery by-products. From the 1920s to the 1940s, familiar man-made products like nylon, polystyrene, and polyvinyl chloride (PVC) were developed. Synthetic dyes, paints, and medicines were invented.

Today, petrochemical products are everywhere. They are very useful, but they also have some problems. People throw away a lot of plastic products because they are inexpensive. One problem with plastics is that generally they do not rot or break up like natural materials. Plastic bags are already polluting oceans and killing wildlife. They cannot easily be remelted and reused.

Scientists and petrochemical manufacturers continue their work to develop safe and useful products.

● Language spot

and, but, because

- We use *and* to join two sentences. It shows that we are giving additional information.
  It was discovered in prehistoric times.
  It's commonly used today.
  *It was discovered in prehistoric times, **and** it's commonly used today.*
  The first petrochemical factory was built in 1872.
  It made carbon black from natural gas.
  *The first petrochemical factory was built in 1872, **and** it made carbon black from natural gas.*

- We use *because* to join two sentences. It shows why something happens or is true.
  It became possible to make large amounts of it cheaply. Natural gas was plentiful and inexpensive.
  *It became possible to make large amounts of it cheaply **because** natural gas was plentiful and inexpensive.*

  People throw away a lot of plastic products.
  They are inexpensive.
  *People throw away a lot of plastic products **because** they are inexpensive.*

- We use *but* to join two sentences. It shows that the additional information may be unexpected.
  They are very useful.
  They also have some problems.
  *They are very useful, **but** they also have some problems.*

  Carbon black wasn't a new product.
  Using a big factory was a new way of making it.
  *Carbon black wasn't a new product, **but** using a factory was a new way of making it.*

1 Complete the sentences. Use *and*, *but*, or *because*.

1 I was late this morning _____ I had a problem with my car.

2 We repaired the compressor yesterday, _____ it stopped working again this morning.

3 We started work at 9.00, _____ we finished at 4.00.

4 I want to go to the meeting, _____ I really don't have time.

5 We'll tidy up the workshop today _____ start work on the pump repair tomorrow.

6 I can't replace the lamp today _____ I haven't got a new one.

2 Write three sentences for each set of sentences. Use *and*, *but*, or *because*. There is more than one correct answer in some cases.

EXAMPLE

I took an umbrella.   *It wasn't raining.*
I didn't take an umbrella.   *I wore my raincoat.*
(and)   *I took an umbrella, and I wore my raincoat.*
(but)   *I took an umbrella, but it wasn't raining.*
(because) I didn't take an umbrella because it wasn't raining.

1 We called the medic.   Juan injured his hand.
  I cut my finger.   It wasn't serious.

  a (and) _____

  b (but) _____

  c (because) _____

2 We replaced the gasket.   We cleaned the spark plug.
  It's running much better.   It's making a funny noise.

  a (and) _____

  b (but) _____

  c (because) _____

3 We aren't using this tank.   It's damaged.
  We're using this tank.   It isn't damaged.

  a (and) _____

  b (but) _____

  c (because) _____

>> Go to **Grammar reference** p.124

composite fibre (n) a thin, strong thread or string made from two or more other materials, for example polypropylene and polyethylene. Composite fibres are often made into fabric.

carbon fibre (n) a very thin, strong thread or string, usually 0.005–0.010 mm in diameter, made mostly from carbon molecules. Carbon fibres are made into very strong, light products.

Spunbond is a fabric made from composite fibre.

Listening

Factory and product description

1 Use the words to complete the text.

polyethylene	near Tokyo	Goi Factory
polypropylene	Chisso Petrochemical Corporation	

Company: _____ 1

Plant: _____ 2

Location: _____ 3

Main products: _____ and _____ 4

2 🎧 Listen and check your answers.

Chisso Petrochemical's Goi Factory

3 🎧 Listen again. Tick (✓) the words you hear.

Polyethylene
1 18 million tonnes per year
2 80 million tonnes per year
3 packaging material
4 packing material

Polypropylene
5 ropes
6 car parts
7 shopping bags
8 fabrics
9 containers
10 bottles
11 50 million tonnes per year
12 15 million tonnes per year

4 🎧 Listen again. Check your answers.

5 🎧 Listen. Complete the words.

Chisso's Moriyama Plant
m_____1
composite fibres.
It u_____2
the polypropylene and
polyethylene p_____3
at the Goi Plant.
It s_____4 in the
production of spunbond fabric.
Spunbond composite
i_____ u_____5
to make floor carpets for cars,
medical packaging, diapers, very
strong envelopes, and many
other products.

Chisso Petrochemical's Moriyama Plant

6 🎧 Listen again. Check your answers.

Speaking

Describing a petrochemical product

Practise describing a factory and one of its products. Speak in full sentences as in **5** above.

Student A, go to p.111. Student B, see below.

1 Tell Student A about this company.

Company: Arg-Nyl
Plant: San Lorenzo
Location: near Buenos Aires, Argentina
Main product: nylon fabric
Product used for: clothing, shoes, camping tents

2 Listen to Student A. Complete the description.

Company: _____

Plant: _____

Location: _____

Main product: _____

Product used for: _____

USEFUL LANGUAGE

Chisso's Moriyama Plant is . . .

It manufactures . . .

. . . is used to make . . .

toxic chemical (adj) a gas, liquid, or powder that can hurt people

domestic appliance (n) a machine used in the home, for example a dishwasher, toaster, or oven

resin (n) a very thick, sticky liquid often made from polymers

Br E	Am E
at school	in school
left school	graduated from high school

It's my job

1 Read the text. Answer the questions.

1 What's the name of Debbie's company?
2 Which part of the company does she work in?
3 What has she learned to use?
4 Who buys her company's products?
5 What subject has her job taught her about?
6 Which industry will use the product that Debbie tested this morning?

2 Debbie mentions these three tests for strength. Find the name of each test in the text.

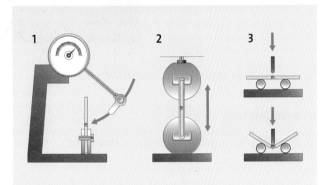

3 Debbie says that the quality of the product she tested this morning must be very high. Why is high quality important in this case?

Debbie Johnson

I'm a test technician for Specialist Plastics Limited. My company makes special polymers – plastics – and I work in the test department. I have been here since I left school, and I have been trained to use most of the test equipment.

We test all of our materials for strength. We bend them in the bend test, we pull them in the tensile test, and we hit them with a hammer in the impact test. We need to see how easily they break. This includes testing them at different temperatures. We also test them with different chemicals. We need to understand how chemicals might change our materials. For example, when we put some of our plastics in sea water, they very become weak. We also have to burn them because some materials make toxic chemicals when they burn. We need to know about that.

Writing

Materials requisition

1 Read the email. Answer the questions on p. 105.

Pietro,

I'm doing some tests next week and I need some polycarbonate pellets. Could you please get 500 kg of our ref PC 180? I want those packaged in 20 kg bags, and I need them on 9 April, delivered to the Teesside lab. Please get them from Plasco, Hitrust (Sizhou), or Yugao Dayu.

Thanks a lot!

George Harvey

ext 3578

My company supplies plastics for larger plastics manufacturers. We also make products for other industries such as aerospace, oil and gas, and domestic appliance companies.

I didn't learn much about chemistry at school, but I've learned a lot about it in this job. There are so many plastics. People use them in so many different ways. And most of them are made from petroleum. It's amazing.

This morning I tested special resins used with carbon fibre to make aircraft wings. We test this kind of product very carefully because the quality must be very high.

1 What material does George Harvey want?
2 How much (what quantity) does he need?
3 What type of packaging does he mention?
4 He names three suppliers. What are they?

2 Read the email again. Complete the form.

> ● A materials requisition form is used to ask your company's buyer to buy something that you need for your work.

MATERIALS REQUISITION

Material: _____	1
Reference number: _____	2
Quantity: _____	3
Packaging: _____	4
Delivery date: _____	5
Delivery location: _____	6
Preferred suppliers: _____	7
Requested by: _____	8
Telephone extension: _____	9

Project

Every day, you use products that contain petrochemicals.
Make a list of these things. Be specific. Include

● clothing
● food preparation and storage
● transport
● electronics
● decorations in your home
● any other ideas you have.

Key words

Nouns
carbon black
molecule
monomer
plastics
polyethylene
polymer
requisition
supplier

Adjectives
inexpensive
man-made
plentiful
prehistoric
synthetic

Verbs
package
specialize (in)

Look back through this unit. Find five more words or expressions that you think are useful.

Speaking activities

Unit 1 p.7

Checking

Student A

Look at this list. Ask Student B *What's in box 1?* Find four things that are wrong.

Items	Part no.
130 washers	W7634
24 screws	R20197
40 bolts	B1208
40 nuts	N7604

Now look at these items and answer Student B's questions.

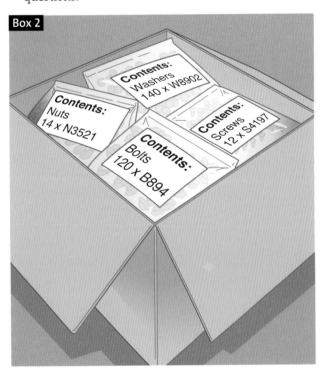

Box 2

Contents:
Washers
140 x W8902

Contents:
Nuts
14 x N3521

Contents:
Screws
12 x S4197

Contents:
Bolts
120 x B894

Unit 2 p.13

Talking about jobs

Student A

Ask questions about Igor Kinsky and complete the information. Then answer Student B's questions about Andrea Farrell.

	Igor Kinsky	Andrea Farrell
Company		a British oil company
Job		helicopter pilot
Where		Aberdeen, Scotland
A typical day		take men and equipment to offshore platforms
Hours per day		12 hours maximum
Start and finish		usually 7 a.m. to 7 p.m.
Like		flying helicopters

Unit 2 p.14

Measuring oil and gas

Student A

a 775
b 53,421
c 1,296,000
d 84,000,000,000

Unit 3 p.19

Making and taking calls

Student A

Conversation 1

You work in Technical Support with George, but he is giving a talk right now. The phone rings. Answer it and complete this message.

Message

To: _____

From: _____

Of: (company/department): _____

Message: _____

_____

_____

Date: _____ Time: _____

Conversation 2

Phone Faisal Hamdi in Human Resources. Does he need any new equipment?

Unit 4 p.23

What does it mean?

Student A

Ask about the signs on the left. Write the meanings. Then answer Student B's questions.

Do not touch

Wear ear protectors

Emergency stop button

Slippery surface

Unit 5 p.33

Discussing specs

Student A

Ask about the R40 radio and complete the information below. Answer B's questions about the SP90.

	SP90	R40
channels	4	
dimensions	120 x 55 x 30 mm	
weight	170 g	
colour	black	
material	hard plastic	
maximum range	10 km	
battery life	40 hrs	
water resistant	yes	
shock resistant	yes	
sand and dust resistant	yes	
separate microphone	yes	
display screen	no	
controls	channel selector knob, volume control, on/off switch, press-to-talk button	

Unit 7 p.41

Describing a pipeline

Student A

1 Describe the location of this pipeline to Student B. Start at the top of the picture.

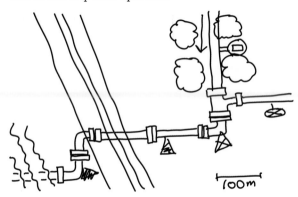

2 Listen to Student B's description of the location of the pipeline. Mark it on the map.

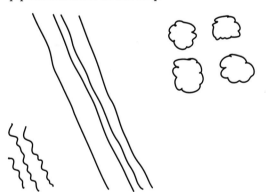

Unit 7 p.44

Measuring pipes

Student A

1 Say these calculations. Student B will write them.

1 $3.14 \times 0.5 \times 0.5 \times 12 = 9.42 \text{ m}^3$
2 $3.14 \times 2 \times 2 \times 24 = 301.44 \text{ m}^3$
3 $3.14 \times 0.75 \times 0.75 \times 3 = 5.2987 \text{ m}^3$

2 Listen to the calculations that Student B says. Write them in numbers.

1 _____

2 _____

3 _____

Unit 8 p.51

Radio conversations

Student A

Radio conversation 1

Call Student B. Find out:

1 Does he have a list of workers on B shift?
2 The name of the electrician _____
3 The name of the engineer _____
4 Is there an Adams on the list?

Radio conversation 2

Answer Student B's call. Answer B's questions about these pressure gauges.

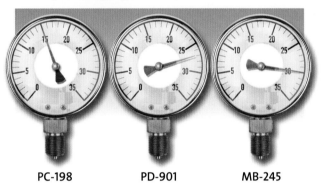

PC-198   PD-901   MB-245

Unit 9 p.68
Describing equipment

Student A

1 Student B has the same pictures, but in a different order. Try to match your pictures (1–9) with Student B's pictures (a–i). Talk with Student B. Do not look at Student B's book. Also exchange information about tank capacity.

EXAMPLE

A *This tank is vertical.*
B *Is it above-ground?*
A *Yes, it is. And it's cylindrical.*
B *OK. That picture is letter b on my card.*
A *Letter b? OK. It's number 1 on my card. What's its capacity?*
B *One thousand eight hundred cubic metres.*

2 After you have matched all nine pictures, check your answers.

Capacity

_____

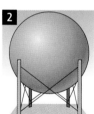

Capacity
15,000 m³

Capacity 1,200 m³

Capacity

_____

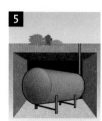

Capacity 1,000 m³

Capacity

_____

Capacity

_____

Capacity
45,000 m³

Capacity 60 m³

Unit 10 p.74
Reporting an incident

Student A

1 You receive a phone call about an incident. Complete the notes about the incident.

Begin by answering the phone: *Control Room, (your name) speaking.*

Type of incident: _____

Location: _____

Injuries: ☐ yes   ☐ no

Situation: _____

_____

Finish the call with *OK, I'll contact emergency services and get a maintenance team right away.*

USEFUL LANGUAGE

Where is it, exactly?
Is anyone hurt?
What's the situation now?

2 Report this incident. Phone Student B.

● It's between tanker bays 3 and 4.
● No one is injured.
● The gas is continuing to leak. You're working to shut off the correct valve.

Student B will answer the phone. You say: *This is (your name). I'm in the bulk tanker loading area. There's a*

_____ *.*

Then answer Student B's questions.

Unit 11 p.80
Saying what's been done
Student A

1 You are a workshop manager. It is Tuesday. Your workers are building a containment for an oil tank. Phone Student B. Ask questions in the Present Perfect.
1 build the base?
2 assemble the containment?
3 put the tank in the containment?
4 weld the containment?

2 Now it is Wednesday. You are on site. Your manager telephones and asks you some questions. Look at the pictures. Answer the questions in full sentences. Use the Present Perfect.

do grinding ✓ check inside ✓

attach the cover ✗

put the tank on the truck ✗

3 Now tell Student B three things you have done today and three things you haven't done today.

Unit 13 p.90
Explaining a process
Student A

1 Listen to Student B. Number the pictures in the correct order.

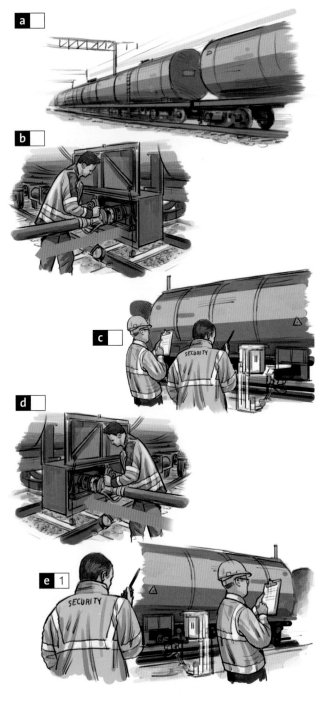

a ☐

b ☐

c ☐

d ☐

e ☐ 1

2 Explain this process to Student B.

Loading crude oil into a bulk tanker

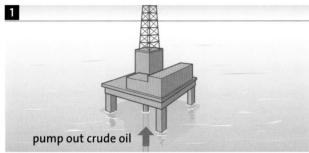

1 pump out crude oil

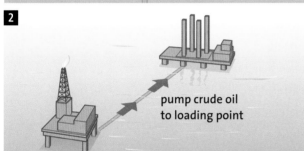

2 pump crude oil to loading point

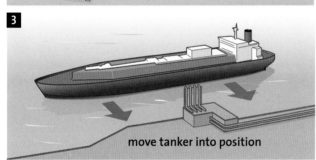

3 move tanker into position

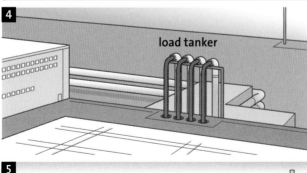

4 load tanker

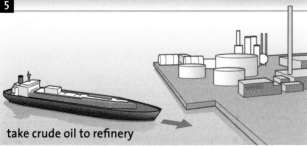

5 take crude oil to refinery

Unit 14 p.98

Explaining an accident

Student A

1 You saw the incident below. Luke Inman has hurt his back. Phone Student B, a medic, to report it. Begin with *There's been an accident.*

8.30 a.m. 12 August preparing to install pipeline, near the main refinery

2 You are the medic. Answer Student B's phone call. Ask for details about the accident. Make notes. Give advice.

Unit 15 p.103

Describing a petrochemical product

Student A

1 Listen to Student B. Complete the description.

Company: _____
Plant: _____
Location: _____
Main product: _____
Product used for: _____

2 Tell Student B about this company.

Company: Ming Hing Carbon Company

Plant: MH Guangzhou Works

Location: Guangzhou, China

Main product: carbon fibre

Product used for: composite fabrics used in cars and airplanes

Unit 2 p.14
Measuring oil and gas

Student B

a 909
b 215,000
c 40,570,000
d 14,000,000,000

Unit 4 p.23
What does it mean?

Student B

Answer Student A's questions. Then ask about the signs on the right. Write the meanings.

Unit 5 p.33
Discussing specs

Student B

Answer A's questions about the R40 radio. Ask about the SP90 and complete the information below.

	SP90	R40
channels		40
dimensions		140 x 56 x 33 mm
weight		230 g
colour		grey
material		metal
maximum range		20 km
battery life		30 hrs
water resistant		no
shock resistant		yes
sand and dust resistant		yes
separate microphone		no
display screen		yes
controls		keypad and display, separate volume control, on/off button

Unit 7 p.41
Describing a pipeline

Student B

1 Listen to Student A's description of the location of the pipeline. Mark it on the map.

2 Describe the location of this pipeline to Student A. Start at the top of the picture.

Unit 7 p.44
Measuring pipes

Student B

1 Listen to the calculations that Student A says. Write them in numbers.

1 _____

2 _____

3 _____

2 Say these calculations. Student A will write them.

1 $3.14 \times 2 \times 2 \times 5 = 62.8 \text{ m}^3$

2 $3.14 \times 0.7 \times 0.7 \times 30 = 46.158 \text{ m}^3$

3 $3.14 \times 0.25 \times 0.25 \times 22 = 4.3175 \text{ m}^3$

Unit 8 p.51
Radio conversations

Student B

Radio conversation 1

Answer Student A's call. Answer A's questions, using information on this list.

Workers on B shift

Name	Job
Albaradei, M	engineer
Andersson, L	control room operator
Alvarez, J	cook
Ashwell, B	mechanical technician
Aston, E	pipe-fitter
Atkins, P	electrician
Azar, S	radio operator

Radio conversation 2

Call Student A. Get this information.

1 Are any gauges showing zero pressure?

2 Are any gauges showing higher than 25? Which ones?

Gauge no.		
Pressure		

Unit 9 p.68
Describing equipment

Student B

1 Student A has the same pictures, but in a different order. Try to match your pictures (a–i) with Student B's pictures (1–9). Talk with Student A. Do not look at Student A's book. Also exchange information about tank capacity.

EXAMPLE

A *This tank is vertical.*

B *Is it above-ground?*

A *Yes, it is. And it's cylindrical.*

B *OK. That picture is letter b on my card.*

A *Letter b? OK. It's number 1 on my card. What's its capacity?*

B *One thousand eight hundred cubic metres.*

2 After you have matched all nine pictures, check your answers.

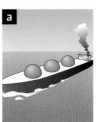

Capacity

_____

Capacity

1,800 m³

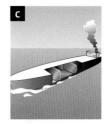

Capacity

39,000 m³

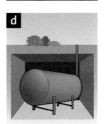

Capacity

_____

Capacity 1,200 m³

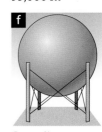

Capacity

_____

Capacity

_____

Capacity 40 m³

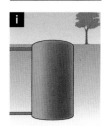

Capacity

75,000 m³

Unit 10 p.74

Reporting an incident

Student B

1 Phone Student A. Report this incident.

- On the south side of the sulphur plant
- Your eyes are burning and there's a very bad smell
- You're moving away from the area

Student A will answer the phone. You say *This is (your name). I'm at the sulphur plant. There's a really bad _____ .*

Then answer Student A's questions.

2 You receive a phone call about an incident. Complete the notes about the incident. Begin by answering the phone: *Control Room, (your name) speaking.*

Type of incident: _____

Location: _____

Injuries: ☐ yes   ☐ no

Situation: _____

_____

Finish the call with *OK, I'll contact emergency services and get a maintenance team right away.*

USEFUL LANGUAGE

Where is it, exactly?

Is anyone hurt?

What's the situation now?

Unit 13 p.90

Explaining a process

Student B

1 Explain this process to Student A.

Loading a bulk tanker train at a refinery

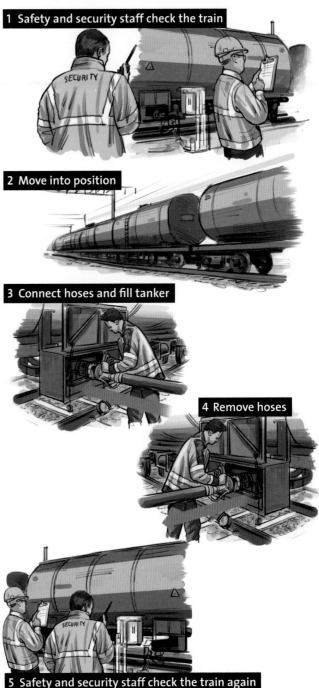

1 Safety and security staff check the train

2 Move into position

3 Connect hoses and fill tanker

4 Remove hoses

5 Safety and security staff check the train again

2 Listen to Student A. Number the pictures in the correct order.

a

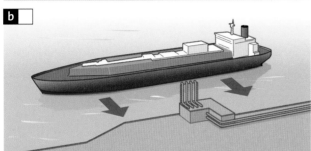

b

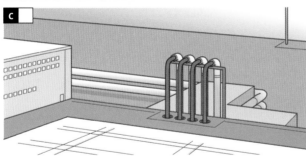

c

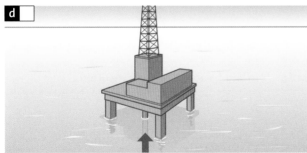

d

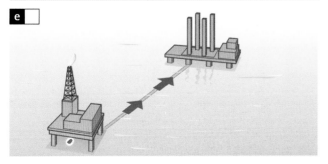

e

Unit 14 p.98

Explaining an accident

Student B

1 You are the medic. Answer Student A's phone call. Ask for details about the accident. Make notes. Give advice.

2 You are the man below. Your arm is broken. Phone Student A, a medic, to report it. Begin with *I've had an accident.*

4.00 p.m. 19 June in the pipe field replacing a valve

Irregular verbs

Infinitive	Past Simple	Past Participle	Infinitive	Past Simple	Past Participle
be	was / were	been	know	knew	known
become	became	become	leave	left	left
begin	began	begun	lose	lost	lost
break	broke	broken	make	made	made
bring	brought	brought	meet	met	met
build	built	built	put	put	put
burn	burnt / burned	burnt / burned	quit	quit	quit
buy	bought	bought	read	read	read
choose	chose	chosen	ride	rode	ridden
come	came	come	run	ran	run
cost	cost	cost	say	said	said
cut	cut	cut	see	saw	seen
deal	dealt	dealt	sell	sold	sold
dig	dug	dug	send	sent	sent
do	did	done	shake	shook	shaken
drink	drank	drunk	show	showed	shown
drive	drove	driven	shut	shut	shut
fall	fell	fallen	sleep	slept	slept
feel	felt	felt	smell	smelt	smelt
find	found	found	speak	spoke	spoken
fly	flew	flown	spend	spent	spent
freeze	froze	frozen	stand	stood	stood
get	got	got / gotten	swim	swam	swum
give	gave	given	take	took	taken
go	went	gone / been	teach	taught	taught
grow	grew	grown	tell	told	told
have	had	had	think	thought	thought
hear	heard	heard	throw	threw	thrown
hide	hid	hidden	understand	understood	understood
hit	hit	hit	wear	wore	worn
hurt	hurt	hurt	write	wrote	written
keep	kept	kept			

Abbreviations

°	degree		LNG	liquefied natural gas
%	per cent		LON	longitude
π	pi		LPG	liquefied petroleum gas
±	plus or minus		m	metre
2D	two-dimensional		m^3	cubic metre
3D	three-dimensional		mm	millimetre
A	amps		μm	micron
a.m.	ante meridian (in the morning)		mPa	megapascal
bbl	barrel		N	north
bpd	barrels per day		N	nitrogen
C	Carbon		no.	number
C	Celsius		NOC	national oil company
co.	company		Ω	ohms
CO_2	carbon dioxide		p.m.	post meridian (in the afternoon / evening / at night)
dd/mm/yyyy	day/month/year			
E	east		PPE	personal protection equipment
g	gram		PTT	press to talk
GPS	global positioning system		PVC	polyvinyl chloride
H	hydrogen		r	radius
HR	Human Resources		R	resistance
IOC	international oil company		S	south
k	kilogram		t	tonne
kPa	kilopascal		UAE	United Arab Emirates
kph	kilometres per hour		UK	United Kingdom
I	current		USA	United States of America
l	litre		V	voltage / volts
LAT	latitude		W	west

Grammar reference

1 *a / an / the*, the verb *be*

a / an

We use *a* and *an* to talk about something in general.

We use *a* + singular noun that begins with a consonant.
a pipeline, ***a*** team, ***a*** department

We use *an* + singular noun that begins with a vowel.
an oil rig, ***an*** effect, ***an*** idea

However, we use *a* before nouns that begin with a 'y' sound, e.g. ***a*** *university*.

the

We use *the* before singular and plural nouns to talk about:
- a specific example of something
  *Muktar is **a** manager.* (= one of several)
  *Muktar is **the** manager of this department.* (= there is only one manager)
- something that is known to everyone present
  *He works at **the** university.* (= everyone understands which university it is)
- something that has been mentioned earlier
  A *new plant has just opened. We will visit **the** plant next week.*
- some countries, regions, rivers, seas, and oceans
  the *UAE,* ***the*** *US,* ***the*** *UK,* ***the*** *Middle East,* ***the*** *Danube,* ***the*** *North Sea,* ***the*** *Pacific Ocean*

The verb *be*

Positive

I	**am ('m)** late.
He / She / It	**is ('s)** late.
We / You / They	**are ('re)** late.

= subject + ***am / is / are***

Negative

I	**am not ('m not)** late.
He / She / It	**is not (isn't)** late.
We / You / They	**are not (aren't)** late.

= subject + ***am / is / are + not*** (***'m not / isn't / aren't***)

Questions	**Short answers**
Am I late?	Yes, I **am**. No, I **'m not**.
Is he / she / it late?	
Are we / you / they late?	

= ***Am / Is / Are*** + subject

We can use question words such as *What* or *How* if we want more specific information than a yes / no answer will give.

What is *your job? ~ I'm a radio operator.*

We can use the verb *be* for:
- nationalities and places of origin
  *The team manager **is** from Dublin.* (= subject + *am / is / are + from* + place)
  *Mr Beyrand and Ms Gougelot **are** French.* (= subject + *am / is / are* + adjective)
  *Gazprom **is** a Russian company.* (subject + *am / is / are + a / an* + adjective + noun)
- introductions and occupations
  *My name**'s** Don Bradman.*
  *This **is** Ranjit Chatterjee. He**'s** your new manager.*
- personal information
  *Your employee number **is** 2173.*
  *What **is** your address?*

there is, there are

We use *there is, there are* to say that something exists. We often use this phrase when describing the contents of an item or a building's facilities.

We use *there is + a / an*, and *there are + some* or a number.

There is *a glossary at the back of this book.*
There are *three restaurants on this site.*

Note that there is no contracted form for *there are*.
NOT ~~*There're three restaurants* ...~~

In questions, we change the order to *Is there ...? / Are there ...?*

Is there *a glossary at the back of the book?*
Are there *two or three restaurants on this level?*

We can also use a question word before *Is there / Are there*.

How many *restaurants are there? ~ There are three.*

2 *do* and *does*, and *Wh-* questions

We use *do* and *does* to form the negative and questions in the Present Simple.

Negative

I / You / We / You / They **do not (don't)** work here.	
He / She / It **does not (doesn't)** work here.	

= subject + ***do / does + not*** (***don't / doesn't***) + infinitive

Questions / Short answers

Questions	Short answers
Do I / you / we / you / they work here?	Yes, I **do**.
Does he / she / it work here?	No, he **doesn't**.

= auxiliary **do / does** + subject + infinitive

We use a question beginning with *do* or *does* to ask a question that requires a yes / no answer.

If we want to find out specific information, we can put a question word before *do* or *does*.

Question words include *who, what, which, when, where, how.*

Where *do you work?*
What *does a well test operator do?*

3 Present Continuous

Positive

I	**am talking**.
He / She / It	**is ('s) talking**.
We / You / They	**are ('re) talking**.

= subject + **am / is / are** + **-ing** form

Negative

I	**am not ('m not) talking**.
He / She / It	**is not (isn't) talking**.
We / You / They	**are not (aren't) talking**.

= subject + **am / is / are + not** (**'m not / isn't / aren't**) + **-ing** form

Questions / Short answers

Questions	Short answers
Am I **talking**?	Yes, I **am**. No, I'**m not**.
Is he / she / it **talking**?	
Are we / you / they **talking**?	

= **Am / Is / Are** + subject + **-ing** form

We use the Present Continuous to talk about what we are doing at the moment. We do not use this tense to talk about routines, jobs, or to give facts about ourselves. For those functions we use the Present Simple.

*We'**re having** trouble with one of the control panels.*
*This machine **isn't working** properly.*
*Why **is** the warning light **flashing**?*

We often use time expressions such as (*right*) *now, at the moment, currently.*

*George is giving a talk **right now**.*
*The team is having a meeting **at the moment**.*

-ing form

The rules for forming the *-ing* form are as follows:
- verb + *-ing*
  talk → *talking*   *work* → *working*
- verbs ending in *-e*:
  live → *living*   *take* → *taking*
  not ~~liveing, takeing~~
- short verbs ending in consonant + vowel + consonant:
  get → *getting*   *stop* → *stopping*

4 Modal verbs *can* and *must*

Modal verbs never change their form and are always followed by the infinitive.

can

We use *can* to talk about ability.

Positive

I / You / He / She / It / We / You / They **can lift** this.

= subject + **can** + infinitive

Negative

I / You / He / She / It / We / You / They **cannot (can't)** lift this.

= subject + **cannot (can't)** + infinitive

Questions / Short answers

Questions	Short answers
Can I / you / he / she / it / we / you / they **lift** this?	Yes, I **can**. No, he **can't**.

= **Can** + subject + infinitive

Can / can't often refer to something that is (not) possible in the circumstances.

*One of the hazards is that the load **can** fall on you.*
*I wear a safety harness, so I **can't** fall very far.*

We also use the question form of *can* to ask for permission and to make a request or ask for help.

Permission	**Can** *we accompany you on the tour?* ~ *Yes, of course. / No, I'm afraid not.*
Help	**Can** *you explain the process to me?*
	Can *I ask a question?*
	Can *you help me prepare this load?*

must

We use *must* to talk about obligation, instructions, and rules.

Positive

I / You / He / She / It / We / You / They	**must listen** carefully.

= subject + **must** + infinitive

Negative

I / You / He / She / It / We / You / They	**mustn't come** into this area without shoes.

= subject + **must + not (mustn't)** + infinitive

We often use *must* and *mustn't* when giving spoken instructions.

*One man **must** always have radio contact with the crane operator.*
*We **mustn't** go beyond this line.*

5 Words in sentences

There are three kinds of sentences: statements, questions, and imperatives.

In statements, the word order is as follows:

subject + verb

In questions, the word order is usually:

verb + subject

In imperatives, there is no subject.
***Take** this to the drilling platform.*
***Don't do** anything yet.*

There are other words that we can use in a sentence, such as nouns, pronouns, adjectives, and adverbs.

Nouns and pronouns

Nouns are the names of things, e.g. *drill, platforms*. Pronouns are words such as *he, it, they* which can be used instead of nouns. We do not use both together.
NOT ~~*The GPS it tells you your exact position.*~~

Nouns and pronouns can be either the subject or the object of the sentence.

*The **job** is hard work. I haven't got a **job**.*
***It** is on the chair. You're sitting on **it**.*

***We** work with **them**.*
***He** is in the same team as **me**.*
but
***It**'s a GPS receiver. You use **it** to find your exact position on the Earth.*

Adjectives

These are words that describe nouns. They go before nouns or after the verb *be*.

*This a **heavy** piece of equipment.*
*The equipment is **heavy**.*

Adverbs

These are words that describe a verb. The position of adverbs varies within the sentence. Adverbs of frequency (*usually, never, sometimes*, etc.) go before most verbs but after *be* and modal verbs. Other adverbs, such as *carefully, well*, often go after the object. Adverbs never go between the verb and the object.

*It **usually** takes a few seconds to do this.*
*You read the data from the GPS unit **carefully** to get the position right.*

Sentences often include phrases using prepositions such as *in, on, at*, to say when or where something happened or to talk about conditions.

*It's hard work because you're carrying things **in hot weather**.*
*I prefer working **at night**.*

6 Adjective forms

We can change adjective forms to modify the meaning of the adjective.

too, not ... enough

We use *too* + adjective and *not* + adjective + *enough* to talk about qualities in a different way.

*The liquid is **too thick**.* (= it needs to be less thick)
*The liquid is **not thick enough**.* (= it needs to be thicker)

We can use these expressions with adjectives that have opposite meanings to make them mean the same thing.

too thin = not thick enough
too dark = not light enough

-er, -est and more, most

We can add -er to the end of an adjective or put more in front of the adjective to make a comparison between two things or people. We add -est or put the most in front of the adjective to make a comparison between more than two things or people. The rules are as follows:

		Adjective	Comparative	Superlative
Short adjective	+ -er / -est	tall	tall**er**	the tall**est**
Adjective ending in -e	+ -r / -st	large	large**r**	the large**st**
Short adjective ending in consonant + vowel + consonant	double the consonant + -er / -est	big	big**ger**	the big**gest**
Adjective of two or more syllables	more / the most + adjective	modern important	**more** modern **more** important	**the most** modern **the most** important
Adjective ending in consonant + -y	change -y to -i + -er / -est	heavy	heav**ier**	the heav**iest**

Let's make the mud **thicker**.
The problem with the pump is getting **more serious**.

7 Countable and uncountable nouns

Nouns can be countable or uncountable. Both types can be used with the.

Countable nouns

These can be singular or plural. In the singular, they are used with a / an or one. In the plural, they can be used with numbers or other expressions such as some or many.

a pipe   three instruments
an inspector   several fittings
one litre

The verb agrees with the countable noun.

The **pipe carries** the oil.
Some **sparks are coming** out of the machinery.

Uncountable nouns

These have no plural form. They are used with expressions such as some or much, but not a / an or numbers. Examples include safety, smoke, and petrol.
NOT   ~~a smoke, two petrols~~

Uncountable nouns always have a singular verb form.

There **is** smoke inside.
Is there much smoke?

8 Comparative sentences

There are several ways of making comparisons.
- comparative form of the adjective + than
  Helicopters are **faster than** boats.
  Offshore work is **more hazardous than** onshore work.

Note that some adjectives have irregular comparative and superlative forms.
good   better   the best
bad   worse   the worst
far   further   the furthest
I think offshore work is **better** than onshore work.
The platform was **further** from land than I realized.

Note that the comparative form of the adjective is followed by than, not that.
not ~~bigger that~~

- as + adjective + as
  We use as … as to talk about two things or people that are equal in some way.
  The platform is **as** big **as** a football field.
  The rooms are great. They're **as** comfortable **as** they are at home.

- not as + adjective + as
  We use not as … as to say that one thing or person has less of a particular quality than another.
  The food is**n't as** good **as** it is at home.
  Onshore work is **not as** hazardous **as** offshore work.

9 Past Simple *be*

We use the Past Simple of *be* to talk about states and conditions in the past.

Positive

I / He / She / It	**was** late.
You / We / You / They	**were** late.

= subject + **was / were**

Negative

I / He / She / It	**was not (wasn't)** late.
You / We / You / They	**were not (weren't)** late.

= subject + **am / is / are + not** (**'m not / isn't / aren't**)

Questions	Short answers
Was I / he / she / it late?	Yes, I **was**. No, I **wasn't**.
Were you / we / you / they late?	Yes, we **were**. No, we **weren't**.

= **Am / Is / Are** + subject

We can use question words such as *What* or *How* if we want more specific information than a yes / no answer will give.

What was the meeting about? ~ It was about the introduction of a new computer system.

We often use the Past Simple of *be* with past time expressions such as *yesterday* and *last …*

*I wasn't at the meeting **yesterday**.*
*We were at the refinery **last month**.*

10 Past Simple

We use the Past Simple to talk about completed actions in the past.

Positive

I / You / He / She / It / We / You / They **cleaned** the spill right away.

= subject + Past Simple

Negative

I / You / He / She / It / We / You / They **didn't clean** the spill right away.

= subject + **did + not** (**didn't**) + infinitive

Questions	Short answers
Did I / you / he / she / it / we / you / they **clean** the spill right away?	Yes, they **did**. No, they **didn't**.

= **Did** + subject + infinitive

To form the Past Simple in the positive, we add *-d* or *-ed* to the infinitive.

live → lived   want → wanted

*I **waited** all day for the delivery.*
*He **closed** the main valve to make it safe.*

Some common verbs, such are *do*, *go*, or *have*, are irregular.

do → did   have → had
go → went   make → made

Note the use of the infinitive in the negative.

*It **didn't arrive** on time.*
NOT   *It didn't arrived on time*.

We often use time expressions with the Past Simple. These can go at the beginning or end of a sentence.

*They completed the refinery **in 1995**.*
*The whole team went to the meeting **on Thursday**.*
***Last week** I worked on a risk assessment with the operations team.*

11 Present Perfect

Positive

I / You / We / You / They	**have ('ve) checked** the pressure.
He / She / It	**has ('s) checked** the pressure.

= subject + **have / has** + past participle

Negative

I / You / We / You / They	**have not (haven't) checked** the pressure.
He / She / It	**has not (hasn't) checked** the pressure.

= subject + **have / has + not** (**haven't / hasn't**) + past participle

Questions	Short answers
Have I / you / we / you / they **checked** the pressure?	Yes, I **have**. No, I **haven't**.
Has he / she / it **checked** the pressure?	Yes, he **has**. No, he **hasn't**.

= **Have** / **Has** + subject + past participle

Many past participle forms are irregular and need to be learned individually. For example, *be*, *go*, and *take*.

Verb	Past Simple	Past participle
be	was, were	been
go	went	been, gone
take	took	taken

We use the Present Perfect to talk about:
- recent actions
  We've taken out the old switch and put a new one in.
  They haven't repaired the faulty lights.
  Have you done the maintenance check?

- our lives up to now, often with *ever* in the question form:
  Have you ever worked in Kuwait? ~ Yes, I have. I worked there last year. / No, I haven't.

We don't use the Present Perfect to talk about a completed action. With the Present Perfect, there is always a link with the present.

12 *will*

Positive

I / You / He / She / It / We / You / They **will ('ll) check** the reports.

= subject + **will ('ll)** + infinitive

Negative

I / You / He / She / It / We / You / They **will not (won't) check** the reports.

= subject + **will + not (won't)** + infinitive

Questions	Short answers
Will I / you / he / she / it / we / you / they **check** the reports?	Yes, they **will**. No, they **won't**.

= **Will** + subject + infinitive

We use *will* when we:
- decide what to do, often in response to a particular situation:
  This belt is noisy. ~ OK, I'll tighten it.
  The mechanic's coming to look at that part. ~ I won't touch it until he gets here, then.
- talk about the future in general:
  The new bearing will arrive tomorrow.
  Will you be here for the meeting?

We often use *will* with future time expressions, such as *later, tomorrow, next …*

*I'll check the part again **later**.*
*We'll reinstall the pump **tomorrow afternoon**.*

13 **The Passive**

We use the Passive to explain actions or processes. It generally isn't important who does the action. It is the action that is the most important element.

Passive

The crude oil **is stored** in these tanks. (= this is the process; it doesn't matter who stores them)
The refinery and pipes **are hidden** from the village by trees.

= subject + present simple of *be* + past participle

Active

We use the Active when we know who or what does an action, and we feel that it is relevant or important to give this information.

The crude oil **travels** along these pipes into the tanks.
The refinery **uses** river water for cooling the machinery.

= subject + verb

When describing a process, we can sometimes choose to use either the Active or the Passive. In this case, we often use *by* with the Passive to say who does the action.

Active	*A bridge **connects** the refinery to the main road.* *Tankers **bring** crude oil to the refinery.*
Passive	The refinery **is connected** to the main road **by** a bridge. Crude oil **is brought** to the refinery **by** tankers.

14   *if / when / in case, Past Continuous*

if, when

We use *if* and *when* to talk about situations that we expect to happen. Of the two, *when* indicates greater probability.

When *someone is sick or injured, I take care of them.* (= this is a situation that is quite common)
If *there's a fire, we follow a fire-fighting plan.* (= this situation doesn't happen on a regular basis)

in case

We use *in case* when making plans for situations that happen more infrequently, such as an emergency.

We have an evacuation plan **in case** *we need to get everyone off the rig quickly.*

Past Continuous

Positive

| I / He / She / It | **was working**. |
| You / We / You / They | **were working**. |

= subject + **was / were** + **-ing** form

Negative

| I / He / She / It | **was not (wasn't) working**. |
| You / We / You / They | **were not (weren't) working**. |

= subject + **was / were + not** (**wasn't / weren't**) + **-ing** form

Questions / Short answers

Questions	Short answers
Was I / he / she / it **working**?	Yes, I **was**. No, I **wasn't**.
Were you / we / you / they **working**?	Yes, we **were**. No, we **weren't**.

= **Was / Were** + subject + **-ing** form

We use the Past Continuous to describe something that was happening over a period of time in the past.
The fire **was burning** *fiercely.*
I'm sorry. I **wasn't listening**.
Were *you* **training** *to be a medic at the time of your accident?*

We often use the Past Continuous with the Past Simple to describe something that was happening when another action interrupted it.
He **was working** *on a ladder* **when** *he* **fell** *off.*

Fortunately, I **wasn't walking** *near the ladder* **when** *he* **dropped** *the toolbox.*
Were *they* **working** *at the refinery* **when** *the explosion* **happened**?

15   *and, but, because*

We can use *and, but,* and *because* to join two sentences. The linkers *and, but,* and *because* have different meanings.

and

We use *and* to give additional information.

Compare:
Polyethylene is the most commonly used polymer in the world. It is used as a packaging material.
and:
Polyethylene is the most commonly used polymer in the world **and** *it is used as a packaging material.*

but

We use *but* to contrast two ideas or to show that the second idea is unexpected.

Compare:
Polypropylene is also used in packaging. It is used in many other products too.
and:
Polypropylene is also used in packaging, **but** *(it) is used in many other products too.*

because

We use *because* to explain why something happened or why something is true.

Compare:
Polyethylene is important. It is the most commonly used polymer in the world.
and:
Polyethylene is important **because** *it is the most commonly used polymer in the world.*

Listening scripts

Unit 1

It's my job

Hi. My name is Khaled. I am from the UAE – that's the United Arab Emirates. I am a technician with an oil company here. I like my job because every day is different.

Today I'm in a team of five technicians at a new plant. One man is inside in the control room, and I'm outside with the other three men. One man is from the US, and two are from India. We are from different countries, but we all speak English. We use radios to speak to the man in the control room.

Most people in the company are Emirati, but there are many other nationalities too – American, British, Canadian, Egyptian, Indian, and many more. I like meeting foreign people and practising my English.

Listening

T=technician, E1=employee 1,
E2=employee 2, S=storekeeper

Conversation 1

T Excuse me.
E1 Yes?
T Where's the store?
E1 Er . . . I'm not sure. I think it's over there in building two.
T OK. Thanks.

Conversation 2

T Excuse me.
E2 Hi.
T Where's the store?
E2 It's over there. Room 103.
T Thanks.

Conversation 3

S Can I help you?
T Yeah, I need sixteen of these bolts.
S Sorry?
T Sixteen of these bolts.
S Do you know the part number?
T PV3764.
S Could you say that again, please?
T PV3764.
S Is that PV or BV?
T PV . . . 3764.
S OK. I need your employee number.
T That's 0725.
S 0725. OK.

Conversation 4

S There aren't any here. But I can get some from the main store. Can you call me in half an hour?
T Sure. What's the number?
S 784522.
T 784552?

S No, 522.
T 784522. OK, I'll call you later.
S Right.

Speaking

A What's in the box?
B There are some bolts.
A How many?
B Twenty.
A Good. What's the part number?
B PD790.
A What's that number again?
B PD790.
A The list says PD798. They're the wrong bolts.

Writing

Hi there. Welcome to Fire and Safety. I'm your new manager. My name's Don Bradman. Now, er, you need to fill in this form. You have a pen? Right. Your name first, that's first name and family name . . . OK. Employee number. Ah, your employee number . . . Your employee number is 2178 . . . 2178. OK? . . . er, manager – that's me Don Bradman – That's Don, D-O-N, Bradman, B-R-A-D-M-A-N. OK. Good. Just fill in the rest and sign your name at the bottom.

Unit 2

It's my job

I=interviewer, S=Steve

I Who do you work for, Steve?
S I work for a Canadian oil company.
I What's your job?
S I'm a well test operator.
I And where do you work?
S I work in lots of different places, all over Canada.
I Lots of different places?
S Yeah. The company has oil wells all over the country. We go to an oil well for a few days or maybe a few weeks. Then we move on to a different well.
I Who is 'we'? Do you work in a team?
S Yeah. A well-testing crew has three people: a supervisor, an operator, and an assistant operator. At first I was an assistant operator. Now I'm an operator.
I I see. What do you do on a typical day?
S Well, usually we do tests on new wells. First we prepare the test equipment. Some of it's heavy equipment, so it's hard work. Then we do tests – a lot of different tests – and record data on a computer.

I How many hours do you work?
S Do you mean hours per day?
I Yes.
S We work twelve hours a day.
I Twelve hours. When do you start and finish?
S We start at seven a.m. and finish at seven p.m. It's a long day, but it's OK. I like the job.
I Why do you like the job?
S I like working outside. And I like seeing different places. So it's a great job for me.
I One last question: what skills do you need for this job?
S Well, it's hard work, so you need to be fit. Uh . . . And you need to be good with numbers . . . And you need to be careful – I mean careful about safety, and careful reading numbers and recording them.

Listening

There are some very big numbers in the oil and gas industry.

The world uses about 85 million barrels of oil per day. A barrel is 159 litres. So that's more than thirteen billion litres a day. Thirteen billion litres a day is about 560 million litres per hour.

So oil companies need to produce a lot of oil and they need to produce it fast.

There are about 40,000 oil and gas fields in the world. Most of them are small fields, but some are very big. The biggest is the Ghawar field in Saudi Arabia. This very big field is 280 km long and 30 km wide. The Saudi national oil company, Saudi Aramco, operates the field and produces about five million barrels of oil a day. That's a lot of oil! Five million barrels is 790,000 cubic metres: 790,000 cubic metres every day.

Ghawar also produces about 57 million cubic metres of natural gas per day.

Unit 3

Listening

Conversation 1

O=Omar, M=Mike

M Hello. Technical Support.

O Hi. It's Omar in the control room here. Is that George?

M No. George is giving a talk right now. This is Mike speaking. Can I help?

O Well, we're having trouble with one of the control panels.

M What's the problem?

O The gauges aren't working properly.

M Is the warning light flashing?

O Yes, it is.

M OK. I'll come and look at it.

Conversation 2

F=Faisal Hamdi in the HR department, B=Bill

B Hello. Technical Support. Bill speaking.

F Can I speak to the shift supervisor, please?

B He's talking on the other phone. Can I take a message?

F Oh, yes. Thank you.

B Your name and department, please?

F My name is Faisal Hamdi. I'm phoning from Human Resources.

B Faisal Hamdi . . . from HR. OK. And the message?

F Please ask him to call me. Uh, it's about the new technicians. Can he call me today, if possible?

B OK. So the message is: Please call . . . about the new technicians, . . . today if possible.

F Yes, that's right.

B And your number?

F My number is 2233.

B OK.

F Thank you very much. Goodbye.

B Goodbye.

Pronunciation

Exercise 1

1 Europe
2 Qatar
3 business
4 because
5 Iran
6 prefer
7 company
8 industry
9 Africa
10 example
11 producer
12 important

13 UAE
14 CO_2
15 Middle East
16 petrochemical
17 environment
18 refinery

Exercise 3

1 countries
2 prices
3 people
4 before
5 produce
6 reasons
7 per cent
8 expensive
9 Arabia
10 employment
11 increasing
12 separate
13 chemicals
14 ethylene

Number talk

1

A Hey, what's 54 divided by 9?

B 54 divided by 9? That's 6, isn't it?

A Er . . . Yeah.

2

A OK. Let's add up these numbers: 31 plus 14 . . . plus 24.5.

B 31 plus 14 plus 24.5 . . . equals . . . 69.5.

3

A 380 minus 45.3. What does that come to?

B 380 . . . subtract 45.3 . . . I make that 334.7.

A 334.7. I make it that too.

4

A What's 15% of 3,000?

B Huh?

A 3,000 times 15%. Is that 450?

B Er . . . 3,000 times 15% equals . . . 450. That's right.

5

A What's the square root of 81?

B The square root of 81. You know that!

A Come on. What is it?

B 9!

A Oh yes. Of course.

Unit 4

It's my job

Hi. My name's Danny. That's me in the picture near the top of the rig. I often work in high places. It looks dangerous, doesn't it? Well, maybe you can't see my safety harness. I always wear a safety harness, so I can't fall very far.

Still, a lot of people can't go up high, but I love it! How about you? Would you like my job?

I'm a rigger, by the way. What do riggers do? Well, riggers lift things and move things – heavy loads, like big pipes and big machines. First we estimate the weight and the size of the load. Then we decide how we can move it. Sometimes we erect special lifting equipment, and sometimes we work with crane operators.

When riggers work with crane operators, we prepare the load: I mean we put the load in the sling, and then the crane lifts it.

There are a lot of riggers in the oil and gas industry. We're everywhere! Why? Because there's always heavy equipment that needs lifting and moving.

I work for a good company. Safety is important to them. Every day the supervisor talks about safety. There are lots of hazards in my job, so safety is important to me too.

Listening

S=supervisor, T1=trainee 1, T2=trainee 2, T3=trainee 3, T4=trainee 4

S OK. Listen everybody. Today's toolbox talk is about working with cranes. You know cranes can be dangerous. So tell me: what hazards are there?

T1 The load can fall on you.

S Right. So what's the safety rule?

T1 Don't stand under the load.

S Right. Never stand under a load. And wear a hard hat at all times. Another hazard?

T2 Loads can swing left and right.

S Yeah. So what do you do? Do you put your hand on it – try to stop it swinging?

T2 No. You mustn't do that. It's very dangerous. You must never try to stop a swinging load.

S Good. What else can go wrong?

T2 You can lose your fingers!

S That's right! Be careful where you put your hands. You don't want your fingers going up with the load!

Ts Right! Yeah! Ugh!

T4 Excuse me. Can I ask a question?

S Sure. Go ahead.

T4 What can I do in an emergency? I mean, how can I tell the operator to stop lifting?

S Good question: the crane operator can't hear you, so how can you stop him? One answer is hand signals. You know the emergency stop signal – both arms out, left and right. The other answer is radio. One man must always have radio contact with the crane operator.

T4 OK.

S Any other questions? No? Right. Let's go.

Unit 5

It's my job

I work in a seismic crew. I place the geophones. That's my job. We place the geophones before the other crews arrive – the vibrator crews and the recording crew. Then they arrive and they do their work, and then we remove the geophones.

We must put the geophones in the right place – that's very important. So we all have a GPS unit. That's a handheld electronic gadget, like the sat nav in your car. The GPS tells you your exact position. We read the data carefully to get the position right.

The other crews start work when the geophones are ready. The operator in the recording truck talks to the vibrator crews by radio. He tells them to start the vibrators, and he records the seismic data. After that, we pick up the geophones, and then we move to a new location.

This job can be hard work. You're walking a lot and carrying heavy things – in hot weather sometimes, and in difficult places – like mountains and deserts. So you must be fit. I like the job. I like it for two reasons: I love being outside and seeing different places. And I like working in a team. And the money's good too. That's three reasons, isn't it?!

Pronunciation

Exercise 1

Example

We <u>must</u> put the <u>geophones</u> in the <u>right place</u>.
1 That's <u>very important</u>.
2 So we <u>all</u> have a <u>GPS</u> unit.
3 The <u>GPS</u> <u>tells</u> you your <u>exact position</u>.
4 We <u>read</u> the data <u>carefully</u> to <u>get</u> the position <u>right</u>.

Exercise 5

1 This <u>job</u> can be <u>hard work</u>.
2 You're <u>walking</u> a lot and <u>carrying heavy things</u>.
3 So you <u>must</u> be <u>fit</u>.
4 I <u>like</u> the job.
5 I like it for <u>two reasons</u>.
6 I love being <u>outside</u> and <u>seeing different places</u>.
7 And I like <u>working</u> in a <u>team</u>.
8 And the <u>money's</u> good <u>too</u>.
9 That's <u>three</u> reasons, <u>isn't</u> it?!

Listening

Everyone in a seismic crew uses a GPS receiver. GPS stands for Global Positioning System. You use it to find your exact position on the Earth. You can find your position even in the desert or on the sea. And we use it to navigate. Navigate means find your way to other positions. Other positions are called waypoints.

OK, now listen. This is how to navigate. Before your trip, you enter and save the coordinates of all the waypoints. *Waypoints* means the places you want to go to. OK? I'll show you how to do that later.

OK, you're ready to start your trip. The first thing is to find your position. So turn on your GPS to find your position. Now the GPS needs radio signals from three satellites. So wait until it receives signals from three satellites. This usually takes a few seconds or maybe a minute. When it receives the signals, it shows the coordinates of your position. Now it's ready to navigate. So, select the first waypoint. Waypoint 001 for example. Then select GOTO, and you'll see a pointer on the screen. That's your bearing. Follow the pointer to the waypoint. OK? Right. Now let's try it . . .

Unit 6

Kick off

Drilling mud is a mixture of water, clay, and other materials. The mud pump pumps mud from the mud tank into the top of the drill string. The mud flows down inside the drill string to the bit. It cleans and cools the bit. Then it flows up the hole and carries rock cuttings up with it. The mud and cuttings go to the mud screen. The mud screen separates the cuttings from the mud. The mud flows through to the mud tank below.

Listening

Problem 1

A Hey. We have a problem.
B What is it?
A The cuttings aren't coming up.
B They aren't coming up to the surface?
A Yeah. The mud's not bringing them up. It's too thin.
B Is the mud mixer working?
A Yes, it is.
B OK. Let's make the mud thicker.
A Should I add clay?
B Yeah. Add 250 kilos of clay.
A Right. 250 kilos.

Problem 2

A Listen. That mud pump is very noisy. There's something wrong with it.
B Yeah. You're right. It shouldn't be like that. It's working too hard.

A Why's it doing that?
B I guess it's because the mud's too thick.
A Too thick?
B Yeah. It's too thick, so the pump has to work really hard.
A Should we make it thinner?
B Yes. Just a bit. Add 2,000 litres of water.
A OK.
B Add it slowly. Not too fast.
A OK.

Problem 3

A Look. That drilling floor isn't safe.
B Why's that?
A There's mud on the floor. I mean a lot of mud. Somebody might slip.
B OK. Let's make it safer. Hey, Dan! Clean the drill floor, right now.
C Should I use water?
B Yeah, use water, and clean all the mud off.
C OK. I'm on it.

Pronunciation

1	roughneck	5	crew
2	dirty	6	operate
3	senior	7	control
4	older	8	heavier

Unit 7

It's my job

There's a big oil and gas industry in Brazil. We also produce a lot of ethanol. So I'm always busy!

Most metal pipes and fittings are welded. This means that pipe-fitters and welders work closely together. The pipe-fitters read plans for pipe systems, cut and prepare pipes, lay them out, and put all the parts together. They also drill holes for instruments (flow meters, for example) and they assemble flanges, elbows, and tees. Then I do my work. I weld together sections of pipe. After I weld the pipes, the pipe-fitters assemble them. They use bolts to join the flanged joints. Then inspectors inspect and test the pipes. Finally, workers paint and sometimes insulate the pipes.

Welders always have to be careful of electric shock, burns to the skin and eyes, and smoke. Where possible we work in the workshop but a lot of work is out on site. Sometimes I have to work high up or in confined places, for example inside a pipe, so safety is really important.

Listening

H=health and safety officer, P1=pipe-fitter 1, P2=pipe-fitter 2, P3=pipe-fitter 3

H There are six main hazards for welders. Can you name them?

P1 Electric shock.

H Right. So what do we do?

P2 Weld dry. Don't stand in water.

P3 And wear leather shoes and always wear gloves.

H Right. We also check our equipment often. We don't use damaged equipment. We switch off equipment when we aren't using it. Another hazard?

P3 Gas cylinders. Gas cylinders can explode.

H Correct. So how do we stay safe?

P1 Don't drop them!

H Right. How?

P2 Always secure the cylinders. And always move them safely.

H OK. And the three steps before moving?

P2 Close the valve, remove the regulator, and replace the valve cap. Then use a cart to move the cylinder.

H Right. And always close the valve when you go on break or at the end of the day. Also, you should always wear your safety glasses when you're working. OK, that's two hazards. What else?

P3 Arc rays. They burn eyes and skin.

H Precautions?

P1 Cover skin and eyes. Never look at the spark. Always use a welder's helmet and gloves.

H Right. Those things also protect us from arc sparks. Hot sparks can burn clothes and start fires. So wear your protective clothes. Cotton trousers are good. And no pockets! Pockets catch sparks. Another hazard?

P2 Smoke. Smoke from welding can be dangerous.

P1 So we use respirators. And we always know the material we're welding.

H That's right. And indoors, we always use the ventilation system. OK, there's one more hazard on my list. Trips and falls. You work in confined spaces, sometimes underground, sometimes high up. So what do you do?

P3 Always think about where you are. Wear a safety harness.

P2 Keep the work area clean and tidy.

H Right.

Number talk

Exercise 3

1 Three point one four times point zero two two times point zero two two times twelve point four equals point zero one eight eight cubic metres.

2 Three point one four times point five five times point five five times five hundred sixty-five equals five hundred thirty six point six six five three cubic metres.

3 Three point one four times one point two times one point two times twenty two thousand three hundred equals one hundred thousand eight hundred thirty two cubic metres.

4 Three point one four times one point eight times one point eight times six hundred forty thousand equals six million five hundred eleven thousand one hundred four cubic metres.

Exercise 5

Student A

1 Three point one four times point five times point five times twelve equals nine point four two cubic metres.

2 Three point one four times two times two times twenty four equals three hundred and one point four four cubic metres.

3 Three point one four times point seven five times point seven five times three equals five point two nine eight seven cubic metres.

Student B

1 Three point one four times two times two times five equals sixty-two point eight cubic metres.

2 Three point one four times point seven times point seven times thirty equals forty-six point one five eight cubic metres.

3 Three point one four times point two five times point two five times twenty-two equals four point three one seven five cubic metres.

Unit 8

Language spot

1 Offshore work is more hazardous than onshore work.

2 The platform is as big as a football field.

3 The top of the derrick is higher than a twenty-storey building.

4 Drilling platforms are not as big as this.

It's my job

Part 1

I=interviewer, D=Dave Bristow

I What does an instrument technician do?

D Well, offshore platforms have a lot of instruments and instrument systems – everything from simple gauges to electronic and computer systems. They're for measuring, recording, and controlling variables – variables like pressure, flow, temperature, level, and so on. In my job, I install, maintain, and repair these instruments. I inspect and test them regularly and adjust them if necessary. I test electrical circuits too. If there's a problem, I diagnose the problem and solve it.

Part 2

I What's it like living on a platform?

D Well, I only live here for two weeks at a time. We work two weeks and then we have two weeks' leave. We work twelve hours a day for fourteen days, so it's harder than other jobs. At the end of the day, you can rest, watch TV, watch films, go to the gym, read a book. The accommodation is OK. The rooms are small but comfortable. There are two people per room. The food's good – well, not as good as home food, but good.

I How does it compare with onshore work?

D For me, it's better than onshore work. The pay is good, and I get two weeks' leave every month! But it's not good for everybody. I mean it's a long day, and you can't see your family and friends for two weeks.

Listening

M=Martin, D=Dave

M Hello, Dave. This is Martin again. Over ... Dave. Do you read? Over.

D This is Dave. Go ahead, Martin. Over.

M I'm in the control room. Are you in the process area? Over.

D Affirmative. Over.

M Can you see the gauge? Over.

D Negative. Is it P324? Over.

M Negative, Dave. The gauge is PD24. That's Papa Delta Two Four. Over.

D Stand by. ... OK. I see it. Pressure is five bar. Over.

M Say again. Over.

D Pressure reads five bar. Over.

M The reading here is three. Over.

D Do you say three? Over.

M That's correct. There's something wrong, Dave. Can you find out what's wrong? Over.

D Affirmative. I'll do it now. Over.

M Great. Call me when you have some information. Over.

D Check. Over.

M Thanks, Dave. Out.

Vocabulary

Exercise 3

1 The employee's name is Pond – That's P for Papa, Oscar, November, Delta.
2 The part number is SF925. That's Sierra Foxtrot nine two five.
3 Go to Building D. That's D for Delta.
4 The web address is cvo.com. That's Charlie, Victor, Oscar, dot com.

Pronunciation

1 instrument
2 inspect
3 platform
4 stand by
5 foxtrot
6 offshore
7 production
8 electric
9 install
10 equipment
11 volts
12 department

Unit 9

Vocabulary

vaporize	consume
vaporization	consumption
vapour	store
liquefy	storage
liquefaction	transport
liquid	transportation
produce	pipe
production	pipe
product	

Number talk

Exercise 2

1 nineteen seventy
2 two thousand and two
3 one point five trillion cubic metres
4 two trillion cubic metres

Listening

Conversation 1

A Were you at the meeting yesterday?
B No, I was too late. Was it interesting?
A Yes. The new operations manager was there.
B Was he at Ras Tanura refinery before?
A Yes, he was.

Conversation 2

A We're busy!
B Are you? Why?
A There was a big problem this morning.

B What was the problem?
A There was a faulty level gauge on one of the main storage tanks. It's OK now.

Conversation 3

A Are you on your way to the warehouse?
B Yes, we are. The cable trays were ready last Friday.
A Oh, really?
B Yes. It was on the materials report.

Speaking

Exercise 1

a a cube
b a cylinder
c a sphere

Exercise 4

a The tank is cylindrical.
b The unit is cuboid.
c The tank is spherical.
d The tower is vertical.
e The arm is horizontal.
f The machine is above-ground.
g The men are underground.
h The pipe is at a 90-degree angle.
i The boat is on a truck.

Unit 10

It's my job

My name's Ahmed Al-Sabah. I work for the Kuwait Oil Company. I'm a safety and environment officer. I work in Al Ahmadi, in Kuwait. I work closely with our contractors. I help them to work safely and reduce environmental problems. I like my work. Every day, every week, is different. Last week, I worked on a risk assessment with the operations and maintenance team. And I visited some construction sites with my manager. We talked to some of the workers. We explained the importance of health, safety, and the environment. It's a big responsibility, but everyone works together. We help each other.

Listening

Conversation 1

A When did it happen?
B It happened last night.
A What did you do?
B We closed the main valve and made it safe.
B Was it a big spill?
A Less than a hundred litres. We cleaned it up right away.

Conversation 2

A There was a problem with noise.

B Yes, the compressor was very noisy.
A Did they build the new enclosure?
B Yes, the maintenance team finished it yesterday.
A Did it work?
B Yes, it worked very well. It really reduced the noise.

Conversation 3

A When did it start leaking?
B It started leaking two days ago.
A Did you get the new gasket?
B No. I waited all day yesterday. The delivery didn't arrive. But David said it's coming today.

Pronunciation

1 happened
2 closed
3 finished
4 worked
5 started
6 waited

Speaking

P=Pat, A=Adeniyi

P Control Room, Pat speaking.
A Pat, this is Ade. I'm at the tank farm. There's an oil spill.
P Where is it, exactly?
A Between tanks 12 and 14.
P OK. Is anyone hurt?
A No, there are no injuries.
P So what's the situation right now?
A The area's safe. The spill is around 300 litres. It's contained in the bund.
P OK, Ade, well done. Go out to the road and I'll contact emergency services and get a maintenance team there right away.

Unit 11

Listening

1
A Have you done the monthly maintenance on the compressor?
B Yes. I've checked the pressure and added oil.
A No problems?
B No problems.
2
A They had a leaky water pipe at the gathering station.
B And?
A Khaled stopped the leak.
B Good.

3

A What have you done about the lights in the car park?
B The switch was broken. We've taken out the old switch and put in a new one.

4

A Are you busy today?
B We've got a team meeting at eight o'clock. At ten o'clock, we start work on pipeline 29.
A What time do you finish?
B Nine o'clock tonight.

5

A We need two men at well 36 tomorrow. They need welding gear. We also need two men here at the workshop.
B OK. Aziz and Stas can go to 36. Iqbal should stay at the workshop.
A Iqbal and . . .
B Iqbal and Halim.

6

A Have you finished the budget?
B Yes.
A Does it look OK?
B Yes. We've spent $20,000 on new workshop equipment this year. Next year, we can spend $25,000.

Number talk

one millimetre
two millimetres
one micron
two microns
point oh oh one millimetres
point oh two five millimetres
plus or minus

Unit 12

Vocabulary

Exercise 1

A How's it going with that pump?
B Fine. We found the problem.
A What was wrong with it?
B The bearing was frozen.
A Have you replaced it?
B Not yet. But we've ordered a new one. It'll be here tomorrow. And we've replaced the hose.
A Why did you do that?
B It was split.
A Oh, OK. So when will it be ready?
B We'll get the bearing tomorrow morning. We'll reinstall the pump tomorrow afternoon.

Exercise 6

1

A The wires are corroded.
B I'll clean them.

2

A The tank is damaged. There's a big dent in it.
B I don't think we can repair that. I'll write a report.

3

A It's not working.
B What's wrong?
A It's frozen. The system is down.
B OK. I'll re-start the system.

4

A Have you fixed it?
B No. It's jammed.
A I'll get the manual.

5

A I can't remove the bolt.
B Why not?
A It's rusted.
B I'll get the angle grinder.

6

A Ah, here's the problem. Look at the gear. It's worn.
B Yes, I see.
A I'll replace it.

7

A See this belt?
B Yes.
A It's loose. So it's noisy.
B I'll tighten it.

8

A What's the problem?
B It's this cap. It's leaking.
A Is it oil?
B Yes, it is.
A I'll check it.

Pronunciation

Exercise 1

1 Turn the cap.
2 Repair the rip.
3 Pull the tab.

Exercise 4

1 belt
2 bolt
3 computer
4 copier
5 cap
6 broken
7 repair
8 problem

Listening

F=Frank, E=Eric, C=Carl, B=Bill

F OK. Eric, what have you got?
E Right. The front office phoned. Their photocopier is jammed.
F Carl, will you look at that, please?
C Sure. I'll check it out this morning. I may need to call the manufacturer's technician.
F Fine. What else, Eric?
E There's a problem with the generator that the welding team is using. The engine is making a funny noise.
F Bill, can you take care of that?
B Sure. I'll do it this afternoon.
F Thanks, Bill. What are you doing this morning?
B I'm reinstalling that pump.
F Oh, have you finished the repairs?
B Yes. We finished yesterday.
F Great. What else, Eric?
E Let's see. It's time for the routine maintenance on the compressor.
F OK, fine. Bill and Carl are busy, so I'll do that this morning myself. And I'll check yesterday evening's reports. Oh, and the new lights for the loading area arrived yesterday, Carl.
C Oh, good. I'll install those this afternoon.
F OK. I'll give you a hand. Eric, what about you?
E I'll be at my desk all day!

Unit 13

Listening

Welcome to Oakton refinery. This refinery turns crude oil into products like kerosene, petrol, and petrodiesel. Before we begin our tour today, I'll explain the organization of the refinery.

1 This is the jetty. Tankers bring crude oil to the refinery. They unload the crude oil here.
2 The crude oil travels along these pipes into the tanks.
3 This area is called the tank farm. The crude oil is stored in these tanks until it is refined. Some of them are 80 metres high. There are over 200 steps to the top.
4 This is the main refinery. This is where the oil is refined in the distillation towers.
5 These pipes take the products out of the refinery. Some of the pipes take kerosene to the airport.

6 The refinery uses river water for cooling the machinery. The used water is returned here, to the salt marsh. It is often cleaner when it is returned than it was when it was taken from the river.

7 The refinery is connected to the main road here. All of the workers come and go this way. Some of our products leave this way in tankers.

8 The admin block is where the offices are. The people who work here manage the people and all of the machinery at the refinery.

9 Oakton is the neighbouring village. The refinery is hidden from the village by trees.

Number talk

1 minus forty degrees Celsius
2 zero degrees Celsius
3 forty-five degrees Celsius
4 thirty-seven degrees Celsius
5 one hundred degrees Celsius

Unit 14

It's my job

My company supplies medics to the oil industry. My job is really three jobs. I'm a medic. I'm a safety officer. And I'm an environmental officer.

As a medic, I look after the health of the workers. I do their physical examinations. When someone is sick or injured, I take care of them. If someone is badly injured or very sick, I arrange evacuation.

As a safety officer, I do training. For example, when new employees arrive, I give them basic health and safety training. I also check equipment and plan for emergencies. If there's a fire, we follow a fire-fighting plan. We also have an evacuation plan in case we need to get everyone off the rig quickly.

As an environment officer, I look after the working environment. If there are problems with noise or waste management, for example, I deal with them. I check noise levels and I deal with any problems that workers have with the working environment.

Listening

Situation 1

A We have a fire here.
B Where are you?
A And . . . he's burned. His hands are burned.
B Where's the fire?
A We're in the workshop. We were welding.
B OK. Is everyone safe?
A Yes.
B Is the fire burning now?
A No. We used the fire extinguisher. We put it out.
B OK. Can he walk? Can the man with the burned hands walk?
A Yes. OK, he can walk. The burn isn't very bad.
B OK, then bring him to me. Bring him to the clinic.

Situation 2

A Are you OK?
B What happened? Is he OK?
A The toolbox fell off. I was working on the ladder. The tools fell. They hit his head.
B Is he unconscious?
A Yes. Look at his head. This is really serious.
B OK, I'll call an ambulance. Is he breathing?
A Yes, he's breathing.
B Hello? Yes, we have a serious head injury here. We're at the Oakton refinery in the tank area. Tank 27. We need an ambulance. It's serious.

Situation 3

A OK, can you take the discharge hose off?
B Ah! My arms!
A Quick, get under the shower.
B Oh.
A We've got a chemical burn in the loading area. The bulk tanker loading area. Caustic soda solution.
C Have you washed the burn?
A Yes, he's in the shower now. I think he's OK. But we're going to need to clean up.

Pronunciation

Exercise 2

1	switch off	6	welding
2	advice	7	water
3	evacuate	8	very
4	activate	9	worst
5	vehicle		

Exercise 3

1 Do you know where it went?
2 Did you get the wheel?
3 We had a problem with a wiper.

Number talk

A fever is a temperature above thirty-eight point five degrees Celsius.

A normal resting heart rate is sixty to one hundred beats per minute.

A normal resting breathing rate is twelve to twenty breaths per minute.

Eighty-five over fifty-five is a low blood pressure. A hundred and fifty over a hundred is a high blood pressure.

Pain is measured on a scale of one to ten. One is very mild and ten is the worst possible.

Unit 15

Listening

Exercise 2

My name is Toru Yamada. I'm a chemical engineer at Chisso Petrochemical Corporation. I work at our Goi Factory, near Tokyo. Our main products at Goi are polyethylene and polypropylene. Polyethylene is the most commonly used polymer in the world. Around the world, 80 million metric tonnes per year are produced. It is used as a packaging material. Polypropylene is also used in packaging, but is used in many other products too. Ropes, car parts, fabrics, and reusable containers are all made with polypropylene. The world produces nearly 50 million metric tonnes of polypropylene per year.

Exercise 5

Chisso's Moriyama Plant manufactures composite fibres. It uses the polypropylene and polyethylene produced at the Goi Plant. It specializes in the production of spunbond fabric. Spunbond composite is used to make floor carpets for cars, medical packaging, diapers, very strong envelopes, and many other products.

Glossary

Vowels

iː	sea	ʊ	look	aɪ	pipe
i	refinery	uː	room	aʊ	ground
ɪ	drill	u	regulator	ɔɪ	oil
e	belt	ʌ	pump	ɪə	area
æ	gas	ɜː	earth	eə	repair
ɑː	plant	ə	tanker	ʊə	pure
ɒ	rock	eɪ	maintain		
ɔː	cause	əʊ	flow		

Consonants

p	petrol	f	fuel	h	hole
b	bit	v	valve	m	team
t	tank	θ	thin	n	engine
d	field	ð	breathe	ŋ	string
k	crane	s	service	l	well
g	gear	z	design	r	rig
tʃ	bench	ʃ	offshore	j	yes
dʒ	geologist	ʒ	precision	w	wave

above-ground /əˈbʌv ˌgraʊnd/ *adj* on the surface of the earth rather than under it

activate /ˈæktɪveɪt/ *v* to make a device start working

adjust /əˈdʒʌst/ *v* to change something slightly to make it better or more suitable

ambulance /ˈæmbjələns/ *n* a vehicle with special equipment, used for taking sick people to hospital

ammonia /əˈməʊniə/ *n* (*symb* **NH₃**) a **gas** with a strong smell, used to make fertilizers and cleaning substances

area /ˈeəriə/ *n* part of a place, used for a particular purpose

asphalt /ˈæsfælt/ *n* a thick black substance, used for making the surface of roads

assess /əˈses/ *v* to examine and judge a situation, person, etc.

barrel /ˈbærəl/ *n* **1.** a large round container with flat ends and curved sides, used for storing **liquids** such as oil
2. (*abbr.* **bbl**) a unit for measuring oil that equals 42 US gallons (= about 159 litres)

bearing /ˈbeərɪŋ/ *n* the direction in which you must travel in order to reach a particular place. **Bearings** are measured in degrees in a clockwise direction from north.

belt /belt/ *n* a band in a machine that turns round in order to turn something else

bent /bent/ *adj* not straight

block /blɒk/ *v* to prevent oil or gas from flowing through a pipe

boil /bɔɪl/ *v* (of liquid) to reach the temperature at which it forms bubbles and becomes **gas**

bolt /bəʊlt/ *n* a strong metal pin like a screw that attaches to a circle of metal (= a nut) to fasten things together

broken /ˈbrəʊkən/ *adj* damaged or no longer working correctly

budget /ˈbʌdʒɪt/ *n* the money that is available to someone and a plan of how it will be spent

bulk tanker /ˌbʌlk ˈtæŋkə(r)/ *n* a ship or truck that carries oil, gas, or petrol in very large quantities

carbon black /ˌkɑːbən ˈblæk/ *n* a fine carbon powder, used to make black paint or ink and some kinds of rubber

carefully /ˈkeəfəli/ *adv* with care and attention

cause /kɔːz/ *v* to make something happen, especially something bad

chemical /ˈkemɪkl/ *n* a particular compound or substance, especially one which has been artificially prepared

circuit /ˈsɜːkɪt/ *n* the complete path that an electric current flows along

circumference /səˈkʌmfərəns/ *n* the distance around a circle or round shape such as a pipe

clean up /ˌkliːn ˈʌp/ *v* to remove rubbish, dirt, etc. from somewhere, such as oil that has spilt because of an accident

cluttered /ˈklʌtəd/ *adj* (of a place) covered with or full of many things, in an untidy way

connect /kəˈnekt/ *v* to join together two or more things

consume /kənˈsjuːm/ *v* to use something, especially **fuel** or energy

containment /kənˈteɪnmənt/ *n* a structure that an oil tank stands in. The containment holds any oil that leaks from the tank and prevents it from spreading to other areas.

contractor /kənˈtræktə(r)/ *n* a person or company that does work or provides goods for another company

control room /kənˈtrəʊl ruːm/ *n* a room that contains equipment for operating the machines in a factory, **refinery**, etc.

convert /kənˈvɜːt/ *v* to change something from one form, system, etc. to another, for example to change sound waves into an electrical signal

coordinates /kəʊˈɔːdɪnəts/ *n* two numbers that are used to describe the position of something on a map

corroded /kəˈrəʊdɪd/ *adj* (of a metal or hard substance) destroyed slowly by chemical action

crane /kreɪn/ *n* a tall machine with a long arm, used to lift and move heavy objects

crane operator /'kreɪn ˌɒpəreɪtə(r)/ *n* a person who controls a crane (= a machine for lifting and moving heavy things)

cubic metre /'kju:bɪk ˌmi:tə(r)/ *n* (*abbr.* **m³**) a unit of volume that equals 1,000 litres

cuboid /'kju:bɔɪd/ *adj* shaped like a cube (= a shape with six square sides like a box)

cylindrical /sə'lɪndrɪkl/ *adj* shaped like a cylinder (= an object like a pipe with long straight sides and two round ends)

damage /'dæmɪdʒ/ *v* to harm or spoil something

damaged /'dæmɪdʒd/ *adj* harmed or spoiled

danger /'deɪndʒə(r)/ *n* the possibility of harm to someone or something

dangerous /'deɪndʒərəs/ *adj* likely to cause harm

deal with /'di:l wɪð/ *v* to take action to solve a problem

defibrillator /di:'fɪbrɪleɪtə(r)/ *n* medical equipment that is used to give the heart an electric shock so that it beats normally

degrees Celsius /dɪˌgri:z 'selsiəs/ *n* (*abbr.* **°C**) a scale of temperature in which water freezes at 0° and boils at 100°

department /dɪ'pɑ:tmənt/ *n* a section of a company or other large organization

deposit /dɪ'pɒzɪt/ *n* a substance that is left somewhere by the flow of water, oil, etc., such as dirt left at the bottom of a pipe

derrick /'derɪk/ *n* a tall structure over an oil well for holding the drill

derrickman /'derɪkmæn/ *n* the person who moves the top part of a **drill string**

design /dɪ'zaɪn/ *v* to create and make plans for a new device, machine, etc.

development /dɪ'veləpmənt/ *n* the process of preparing an oil well for production, for example by building a **pipeline**

diameter /daɪ'æmɪtə(r)/ *n* the width of a circle or any other round object such as a pipe

disconnect /ˌdɪskə'nekt/ *v* to separate two or more things

downstream /ˌdaʊn'stri:m/ *adj* connected with the processing and selling of oil and gas

drill bit /'drɪl bɪt/ *n* the cutting part of a drill

drill string /'drɪl strɪŋ/ *n* a series of pipes that form the main part of a drill, connecting the **wellhead** to the **drill bit**

driller /'drɪlə(r)/ *n* a person who controls a drill and manages the work of the drilling crew (= the people who work on a drill)

drilling company /'drɪlɪŋ ˌkʌmpəni/ *n* a company that drills holes for an oil or gas company

earth /ɜ:θ/ *v* to connect equipment to the ground so that it is protected from the possible flow of electric current (Am E = ground)

eco-hazard /'i:kəʊˌhæzəd/ *n* something that can harm the environment

emergency /i'mɜ:dʒənsi/ *n* a sudden dangerous situation which needs immediate action to deal with it

emergency shower /i'mɜ:dʒənsi ˌʃaʊə(r)/ *n* a shower in a factory or laboratory that is used if there is an accident; also called a safety shower

enclosure /ɪn'kləʊʒə(r)/ *n* an area that is surrounded by a wall and is used for a particular purpose

ensure /ɪn'ʃʊə(r)/ *v* to make certain that something happens

environmental /ɪnˌvaɪrən'mentl/ *adj* connected with the environment (= the natural world in which people, animals, and plants live)

evacuate /ɪ'vækjueɪt/ *v* to make people leave a dangerous building or area

exploration /ˌeksplə'reɪʃn/ *n* the process of finding a source of oil or gas that a company can possibly develop

explosion /ɪk'spləʊʒn/ *n* the sudden violent bursting of something like a bomb

fire engine /'faɪə endʒɪn/ *n* a special vehicle that carries firefighters (= people who put out fires) and their equipment

fire extinguisher /'faɪə ɪkˌstɪŋgwɪʃə(r)/ *n* a device with water or chemicals inside that you use to stop a fire burning

first aid kit /ˌfɜ:st 'eɪd kɪt/ *n* a box containing medicine and equipment that you use for emergency medical treatment

flow /fləʊ/ *n* the steady movement of a liquid in one direction

foreign /'fɒrən/ *adj* in or from a country that is not your own

fractional distillation /ˌfrækʃənl dɪstɪ'leɪʃn/ *n* the process of separating the different substances within crude oil by heating it until it becomes a gas and then collecting the gas and liquids that form at different temperatures

frozen /'frəʊzn/ *adj* 1. (of a screw, etc.) stuck or rusted so that it no longer moves 2. (of a computer) not working or responding so that you cannot move anything on screen

fuel /'fju:əl/ *n* a material that you burn to produce heat or power

fuel oil /'fju:əl ɔɪl/ *n* a type of oil produced from crude oil and used as fuel for ships, trains, etc. as well as for heating buildings

fumes /'fju:mz/ *n* smoke or gas which is dangerous to breathe

furnace /'fɜ:nɪs/ *n* a container like an oven that is heated to very high temperatures so that you can melt iron, etc.

gas /gæs/ *n* any substance that is neither a solid nor a liquid, for example hydrogen and oxygen

gauge /'geɪdʒ/ *n* a device for measuring the amount or level of something

gear /gɪə(r)/ *n* a wheel with teeth (= pointed parts) around its edge that works with other gears to control the speed at which an engine turns something

geologist /dʒi'ɒlədʒɪst/ *n* a scientist who studies the earth, especially by examining the rocks of a particular area to find out if oil or gas is under the ground

geophone /'dʒi:əʊfəʊn/ *n* a device that is used on land for recording **seismic** waves so that you can make a map of the land and rocks in that area

go ahead /ˌgəʊ ə'hed/ *v* used to tell someone that they can begin to do something

guide /'gaɪd/ *v* to move something in a particular direction

hazard /'hæzəd/ *n* something that may be dangerous

heading /'hedɪŋ/ *n* the direction in which you are currently moving

heavy /'hevi/ *adj* weighing a lot

horizontal /ˌhɒrɪ'zɒntl/ *adj* going across and parallel to the ground rather than going up and down

Human Resources /ˌhju:mən rɪ'sɔ:sɪz/ *n* the **department** in a company that deals with employing and training people

hydrocarbons /ˌhaɪdrə'kɑ:bənz/ *n* chemicals that are made of hydrogen and carbon, especially the main substances in oil, gas, and coal

incident /'ɪnsɪdənt/ *n* a bad or unfortunate event such as an accident

increase /ɪn'kri:s/ *v* to make something larger in amount

inexpensive /ˌɪnɪk'spensɪv/ *adj* not costing a lot of money; cheap

injure /'ɪndʒə(r)/ *v* to harm someone physically, especially in an accident

inspect /ɪn'spekt/ *v* to examine something closely to check that there are no problems or errors

inspection /ɪnˈspekʃən/ *n* a close examination to check that there are no problems or errors

install /ɪnˈstɔːl/ *v* to fix equipment into position so that it can be used

instrument /ˈɪnstrəmənt/ *n* a tool or device used for a particular task, especially for technical or scientific work

international /ˌɪntəˈnæʃnəl/ *adj* connected with or involving two or more countries

jammed /dʒæmd/ *adj* not able to move

kerosene /ˈkerəsiːn/ *n* a type of oil made from crude oil and used as fuel for planes and for heating in houses

layer /ˈleɪə(r)/ *n* a sheet or level of rock, soil, etc. that is above or below other sheets or surfaces

length /leŋθ/ *n* the size of something from one end to the other

level /ˈlevl/ *n* the amount or height of something, for example the amount of liquid in a tank

light /laɪt/ *adj* not weighing very much

liquefied natural gas (LNG) /ˈlɪkwɪfaɪd nætʃrəl gæs/ /el en dʒiː/ *n* natural gas such as **methane** that is changed into liquid so that it can be stored or transported more easily

liquefy /ˈlɪkwɪfaɪ/ *v* to become liquid; to make something become liquid

liquid /ˈlɪkwɪd/ *adj* in the form of a liquid; not a solid or a gas

liquid petroleum gas (LPG) /ˈlɪkwɪd pəˈtrəʊliəm ˈgæs/ *n* gas that is obtained from crude oil and made into a liquid under pressure. **LPG** is usually a mixture of propane and butane and is used as fuel for some vehicles or for heating in houses.

load /ləʊd/ *v* to put things on or in a vehicle, a container, etc.

maintain /meɪnˈteɪn/ *v* to keep a machine, a tool, etc. in good condition by checking or repairing it regularly

maintenance /ˈmeɪntənəns/ *n* the act of keeping something in good condition by checking or repairing it regularly

manage /ˈmænɪdʒ/ *v* **1.** to be responsible for organizing a business, a team, etc. **2.** to decide how to use money in a sensible way

man-made /ˌmænˈmeɪd/ *adj* made by people; not natural

medical oxygen /ˌmedɪkl ˈɒksɪdʒən/ *n* pure oxygen that is given to someone to breathe as part of medical treatment

melt /melt/ *v* (of a solid substance) to become liquid as a result of heating

messy /ˈmesi/ *adj* untidy

methane /ˈmiːθeɪn/ *n* (*symb* **CH₄**) a gas without colour or smell, that burns easily and is used as fuel. Natural gas mainly contains methane.

micron /ˈmaɪkrɒn/ *n* (*symb* **μm**) one millionth of a metre (= 0.000 001m)

molecule /ˈmɒlɪkjuːl/ *n* the smallest unit of a chemical substance, consisting of a group of atoms

monomer /ˈmɒnəmə(r)/ *n* a molecule that can join with other molecules to form a **polymer**

motor /ˈməʊtə(r)/ *n* a machine that uses petrol / gasoline, electricity, etc. to produce movement and supply power to a vehicle or device

mud /mʌd/ *n* a mixture of water, earth, and other materials which cools and cleans the **drill bit**

noise /nɔɪz/ *n* sound, especially when it is loud or unpleasant

noisy /ˈnɔɪzi/ *adj* making a lot of noise

offshore /ˌɒfˈʃɔː(r)/ *adj* at sea, not far from the land

oilfield /ˈɔɪl fiːld/ *n* an area of land that has large amounts of oil under its surface

oil well /ˈɔɪl wel/ *n* a hole in the ground that an oil company makes in order to get oil

onshore /ˈɒnʃɔː(r)/ *adj* on the land rather than at sea

operate /ˈɒpəreɪt/ *v* **1.** to use or control a machine **2.** to manage an organization or process

operating company /ˈɒpəreɪtɪŋ kʌmpəni/ *n* a company that controls production of an **oil well**

organize /ˈɔːgənaɪz/ *v* to plan work in an efficient way

package /ˈpækɪdʒ/ *v* to put something into a box, bag, etc. so that you can transport or sell it

petrochemical /ˌpetrəʊˈkemɪkl/ *n* any chemical substance that you obtain from crude oil or natural gas

petrodiesel /ˌpetrəʊˈdiːzl/ *n* a type of fuel made from crude oil (= petroleum) and used in diesel engines

pipeline /ˈpaɪplaɪn/ *n* a series of pipes that carries oil and gas over long distances

plant /plɑːnt/ *n* a large factory that processes oil and gas, produces power, etc.

plastics /ˈplæstɪks/ *n* artificial materials that are made from **polymers**. Plastics can be shaped when heated and are used for making many things.

platform /ˈplætfɔːm/ *n* a large structure standing above water in the sea which provides a base for drilling for oil or gas

plentiful /ˈplentɪfl/ *adj* available in large amounts

polyethylene /ˌpɒliˈeθəliːn/ *n* a common type of plastic that is used for making bags or packaging

polymer /ˈpɒlɪmə(r)/ *n* a substance that is made from a number of the same molecules (= **monomers**) that are joined together. Polymers are used to make **plastics**.

position /pəˈzɪʃn/ *n* the place where a person or thing is located

precision /prɪˈsɪʒn/ *n* very accurate: *a precision instrument*

prehistoric /ˌpriːhɪˈstɒrɪk/ *adj* relating to the ancient past before people kept written records

pressure /ˈpreʃə(r)/ *n* the amount of force that a gas or liquid produces in a pipe or container

processing plant /ˈprəʊsesɪŋ plɑːnt/ *n* a factory that separates the different substances within oil and natural gas

product /ˈprɒdʌkt/ *n* a thing that is made, usually for sale

production /prəˈdʌkʃn/ *n* the process of removing oil or gas from the ground and transporting it

protect /prəˈtekt/ *v* to make sure that a person or thing is not harmed or damaged

pump /pʌmp/ *n* a machine that is used to force liquid, gas, or air into or out of something

radius /ˈreɪdiəs/ *n* the distance between the centre of a circle and its outer edge

react /riˈækt/ *v* to respond to something by behaving in a particular way

record /rɪˈkɔːd/ *v* **1.** to keep an account of facts, measurements, etc. by writing them down or storing them in a computer **2.** (of a measuring device) to show a particular measurement or amount

reduce /rɪˈdjuːs/ *v* to make something less or smaller in size

refine /rɪˈfaɪn/ *v* to make crude oil into petrol, plastic, etc. by separating it into different substances

refinery /rɪˈfaɪnəri/ *n* a place where crude oil is separated into different substances and processed in order to produce petrol / gasoline, plastic, etc.

reflect /rɪˈflekt/ *v* to throw back light, sound, etc. from a surface

regulator /ˈregjuleɪtə(r)/ *n* a device on a machine that automatically controls something such as speed, pressure, etc.

reinstall /ˌriːɪnˈstɔːl/ *v* to **install** something again

remove /rɪ'muːv/ *v* to take something away from a place

repair /rɪ'peə(r)/ *v* to fix something that is broken or damaged

replace /rɪ'pleɪs/ *v* to change something that is old or broken for a similar thing that is newer or better

requisition /ˌrekwɪ'zɪʃn/ *n* a formal written request for something

responsibility /rɪˌspɒnsə'bɪləti/ *n* something that it is your duty to deal with because it is part of your job

rigger /'rɪgə(r)/ *n* a person who prepares or uses equipment for lifting heavy objects

risk assessment /'rɪsk əˌsesmənt/ *n* an examination of the possible dangers in a particular situation before it happens

rock /rɒk/ *n* the hard solid material on the surface of the earth; a piece of this material

roughneck /'rʌfnek/ *n* a skilled person who works on a drill, for example by connecting or separating the pipes in a **drill string**

roustabout /'raʊstəbaʊt/ *n* a man with no special skills who does basic work on an oil or gas rig

rule /'ruːl/ *n* a regulation or principle that tells you what to do in particular situations

rusted /'rʌstɪd/ *adj* covered with rust (= a reddish-brown substance that forms on iron when it is in contact with water and air)

safely /'seɪfli/ *adv* in a way that is not dangerous

safety /'seɪfti/ *n* 1. the state of being safe 2. something that prevents injury or harm: *a safety helmet*

SCBA (self-contained breathing apparatus) /'es siː biː eɪ/ /self kən'teɪnd briːðɪŋ ˌæpə'reɪtəs/ *n* special breathing equipment consisting of a container of air which you carry on your back and a tube and mask through which you breathe the air

schedule /'ʃedjuːl/ or /'skedʒuːl/ *n* a plan or list of all the work that you must do and when you must do each task

seismic /'saɪzmɪk/ *adj* relating to earthquakes or other movements of the earth

separate /'sepəreɪt/ *v* to divide things into different parts or groups

service company /'sɜːvɪs kʌmpəni/ *n* a company that supplies equipment and technical services to other companies

shift /ʃɪft/ *n* a period of time worked by workers in a factory, refinery, etc. where some people work at night and other people work during the day

shock /ʃɒk/ *n* you get an electric shock if electricity suddenly passes through your body

sign /saɪn/ *n* a notice with a picture or writing on it that gives instructions, a warning, etc.

signal /'sɪgnəl/ *n* 1. a movement or sound that you make to give instructions, a warning, etc. 2. a series of electrical waves that carry sounds, pictures, or messages

slippery /'slɪpəri/ *adj* (of an object or a surface) difficult to hold or stand on because it is smooth and wet

solid /'sɒlɪd/ *adj* hard or firm; not in the form of a liquid or gas

specialize (in) /'speʃəlaɪz ɪn/ *v* to concentrate on a particular area of business; to become an expert in something

spherical /'sferɪkl/ *adj* shaped like a sphere (= a figure that is completely round like a ball)

split /splɪt/ *adj* with a tear or crack in the surface

stand by /'stænd baɪ/ *v* used to ask someone to prepare or get ready to do something

stretcher /'stretʃə(r)/ *n* a long piece of cloth with a pole on each side, used for carrying a sick or injured person

supplier /sə'plaɪə(r)/ *n* a person or company that supplies goods

supply /sə'plaɪ/ *v* to provide somebody with something that they need

synthetic /sɪn'θetɪk/ *adj* artificial; made by combining chemical substances rather than made naturally by plants or animals

team /tiːm/ *n* a group of people who work together

Technical Support /ˌteknɪkl sə'pɔːt/ *n* a department in a company that deals with problems relating to computers or technical equipment

technician /tek'nɪʃn/ *n* a person whose job involves looking after technical equipment

thick /θɪk/ *adj* (of a liquid) not flowing very easily

thickness /'θɪknəs/ *n* the distance between opposite surfaces or sides of a solid object

thin /θɪn/ *adj* (of a liquid) containing more water than usual so that it flows very easily

tidy /'taɪdi/ *adj* arranged neatly and with everything in order

tighten /'taɪtn/ *v* to make something become tight or tighter

toolpusher /'tuːlpʊʃə(r)/ *n* the most senior person in a drilling crew who is responsible for managing the staff and the supply of equipment; also known as a rig manager

training /'treɪnɪŋ/ *n* the process of learning the skills that you need to do a job

troubleshooting /'trʌblʃuːtɪŋ/ *n* helping to solve problems in a company or an organization

truck /trʌk/ *n* a large vehicle for carrying heavy loads by road

underground /'ʌndəgraʊnd/ *adj* under the surface of the ground

unload /ˌʌn'ləʊd/ *v* to remove things from a vehicle or ship

upstream /ˌʌp'striːm/ *adj* connected with finding and drilling for oil and gas

valve /vælv/ *n* a device that opens and closes and which is used for controlling the flow of a liquid or gas through a pipe

vaporize /'veɪpəraɪz/ *v* to become gas; to make something become gas

vapour /'veɪpə(r)/ *n* a gas such as steam that is created by the heating of a liquid or solid substance

variable /'veəriəbl/ *n* a number or quantity that can change

vertical /'vɜːtɪkl/ *adj* going straight up or down

vibration /vaɪ'breɪʃn/ *n* a continuous shaking movement

volume /'vɒljuːm/ *n* the amount of space in a container, for example the amount of liquid that a pipe can hold

warn /wɔːn/ *v* to tell someone about a possible danger so that they can avoid it

wave /weɪv/ *n* the form that energy such as sound and light takes as it moves

waypoint /'weɪpɔɪnt/ *n* a place where you may stop during a flight or journey

well head /'welhed/ *n* a structure over the top of a well with equipment for controlling the flow of oil or gas

wire /'waɪə(r)/ *n* a thin piece of metal that can carry an electric current

workbench /'wɜːkbentʃ/ *n* a long table used when working with tools

worn /wɔːn/ *adj* made thinner, smoother, or weaker because of being used or rubbed a lot

OXFORD
UNIVERSITY PRESS

Great Clarendon Street, Oxford OX2 6DP

Oxford University Press is a department of the University of Oxford.
It furthers the University's objective of excellence in research, scholarship,
and education by publishing worldwide in

Oxford New York

Auckland Cape Town Dar es Salaam Hong Kong Karachi
Kuala Lumpur Madrid Melbourne Mexico City Nairobi
New Delhi Shanghai Taipei Toronto

With offices in

Argentina Austria Brazil Chile Czech Republic France Greece
Guatemala Hungary Italy Japan Poland Portugal Singapore
South Korea Switzerland Thailand Turkey Ukraine Vietnam

OXFORD and OXFORD ENGLISH are registered trade marks of
Oxford University Press in the UK and in certain other countries

© Oxford University Press 2011

ISBN: 978 0 19 456965 1

Printed in China

This book is printed on paper from certified and well-managed sources.

ACKNOWLEDGEMENTS

Illustrations by: Peter Bull Art Studio pp.4 (world map), 7 (technicians),
14 (map), 18 (man), 19, 23, 25, 26 (asking), 28 (sound waves), 32, 38, 41, 59,
61, 67 (map), 68 (shapes), 76 (responsibilities), 80 (building an oil tank), 82 (oil
pump repairs/maintenance), 83, 84, 90, 94, 98 (accident), 101, 104 (strength
measurement), 110, 114, 115 (accident); Stefan Chabluk pp.7 (tools),
11 (molecules), 14 (cube), 26 (crane, tank, max load), 34, 44, 48 (gauges),
48 (circuits), 65 (bar chart), 67 (pie chart), 74 (bund), 98 (pie charts), 99,
108 (sketches), 109 (capacity), 111 (accident), 112 (sketches), 113; Paul Daviz
p.68 (cow); Mark Duffin pp.6 (numbers), 22 (safety equipment/safety signs),
24 (safety signs), 42 (welding trolley), 43, 49 (multimeter), 54, 56, 79, 86 (safety
sign), 96 (safety signs), 107 (safety signs), 107 (gauges), 112 (safety signs);
Peters & Zabransky UK Ltd pp.4 (oil field), 6 (conversations), 7 (box), 16 (oil/
gas products), 18 (computer control panels), 27, 28 (oil trap), 29, 40, 52,
65 (flow diagram), 67 (tank outline), 68 (biogas plant), 70 (safety hazards), 73,
74 (cleaning up spill), 77, 78 (metal workshop), 82 (oil pump/problems and
solutions), 87, 92, 106 (box), 109 (gas leak), 111 (crude oil transportation),
115 (crude oil transportation).

Cover image courtesy: (North Sea oil platform/Jeremy Hardie/Riser).

*We would also like to thank the following for permission to reproduce the following
photographs:* Alamy Images pp.68 (Natural gas container/RJH_RF), 68 (Low
loader transporting boat/Justin Kase ztenz), 68 (Construction crane/Patrick
Eden), 68 (Air conditioning unit/Frontline Photography), 70 (Wearing masks
in Beijing/Lou Linwei), 72 (Man in hazmat suit/Stock Connection Blue), 72 (Oil
rig explosion/Pictorial Press Ltd.), 76 (Messy workbench/James Schutte),
76 (Tidy workbench/Terry Smith Images Editorial), 78 (Blacksmith/Caro),
78 (McLean Mill/Chris Cheadle), 78 (Makino CNC industrial metal lathe/
RightImage), 78 (CAD computer screen/Doug Steley A), 80 (Mosquito/Nigel
Cattlin), 80 (Man's hand/itanistock), 88 (Jumbo jet with vapour trails/Richard
Cooke), 96 (Safety shower/Guy Croft SciTech), 100 (Spraying fertilizer of crops/
JAUBERT IMAGES), 100 (Colourful airbeds/Greg Balfour Evans), 100 (Hot glue/
studiomode), 100 (Blister packs of pills/Westend 61 GmbH); Aviation-Images.
com p.64 (Tupolev Tu-155); BP p.l.c. p.48 (drilling engineer), 96-97 (BP logos);
Chisso Petrochemical Corporation, Japan p.103 (Chisso Petrochemical plants);
Corbis pp.10 (Oil riggers/Ted Horowitz), 11 (Geologist/Jack Fields), 12 (Factory
worker/Ken Redding), 13 (Helicopter gunner/Eldad Rafaeli), 16 (Delivering gas/
Richard T. Nowitz), 16 (Engineers testing oil pipelines/Gerd Ludwig), 17 (Power
plant control room/Ko Chi Keung Alfred/Redlink), 24 (Workers moving pipes
on barge/Vince Streano), 35 (Casing crew working on oil rig/C. Bowater),
46 (Offshore drilling platform/Hal Beral), 69 (Man with city background/
Shannon Fagan/Cultura), 70 (Dead fish in polluted water/Shoot), 70 (Polluted
soil/Antoine Gyori/Sygma), 72 (Oil well fire/epa), 72 (Gray whale/Denis Scott/
Comet), 80 (Spider weaving web/William Radcliffe/Science Faction), 80 (Paint
peeling on sign/Peter Johnson), 86 (Sparks/Jason Stang), 88 (1959 Cadillac/L.
O'Shaughnessy/ClassicStock), 89 (Aerial view of oil refinery/John Farmar;
Ecoscene), 91 (Working on oil pipeline/Karen Kasamauski), 91 (Aerial view
of oil pipeline/George Steinmetz), 100 (Lipsticks/Thom Lang); Getty Images
pp.8 (Operating drill/Keith Wood/Stone), 10 (Working checking gauge/Lester
Lefkowitz/Stone), 12 (Worker monitoring natural gas well/Keith Wood/
Stone), 50 (Container port worker/EIGHTFISH/The Image Bank), 64 (Natural
gas-fired power station at dusk/Rich LaSalle), 64 (Bus running on natural
gas/Universal Images Group), 67 (Liquified natural gas tanker/AFP), 80 (Red
ant/Danita Delimont/Gallo Images), 88 (Man walking on empty road/Julio
Lopez Saguar/Photographer's Choice), 88 (Worker climbing gas tank/Alvis
Upitis/Photographer's Choice), 96 (Ambulance/Pat LaCroix/Stone), 96 (Man
in hazardous waste suit/Charles Allen/The Image Bank), 100 (Close up of
rolled carpets); Mark Mason's Studio, Oxford p.103 (spun bound fabric);
Oxford University Press pp.21 (Calculator/Ingram), 33 (two way radio/
Ingram), 68 (Petroleum Storage Tank/Photodisc), 72 (Beach/Brand X Pictures);
Photolibrary pp.5 (Man wearing hard hat/Medio Images/White), 11 (Pipeline/
White), 13 (Worker in warehouse/Image100), 24 (Worker on oil rig crane/
Digital Vision/White), 42 (Welding/Glow Images), 64 (Pan and burner flame/
OJO Images), 64 (Tractor watering field of crops/AmanaImages), 68 (Excavator/
Neil Duncan), 68 (Drilling underground/George Hunter/Superstock),
68 (Crane by old building/Fotosearch), 68 (Pipeline/Corbis), 70 (Boy with
hands over ears/Tetra Images), 74 (Oil platform worker on phone/David
Seawell/Bluemoon Stock), 78 (Welding a tank/Glow Images), 78 (Builder using
power drill/Fotosearch), 81 (Hoses connected to fuel tanker outlets/James
Hardy/Photoalto), 84 (Portable generator/Photodisc/White), 86 (Electrician/
Somos Images), 88 (Cruise liner/Design Pics Inc), 91 (Oil refinery worker/
White), 95 (Paramedic/Image100), 96 (First aid kit/C Squared Studios/White),
96 (Defibrillator/Stockdisc/White), 96 (Oxygen tank/Photodisc/White),
96 (Stretcher and first aid kit/Image Source), 96 (Fire fighters putting out
a blaze/Design Pics Inc), 96 (Fire extinguisher/C Squared Studios/White),
100 (Yellow paint in a paint can/Fancy), 100 (Display rack of clothes/Corbis),
100 (Pile of used tyres/Tetra Images); PunchStock p.88 (Truck on interstate 40/
Photodisc); Reuters Pictures p.72 (Oil leaking from carrier/Ho New); Science
Photo Library pp.42 (Technician welding/Ria Novosti), 103 (Carbon fibre
tubing/Bruce Frisch), 104 (Forensic scientist/Tek Image); Shell International
BV pp.5 (refinery) 16 (technicians), 17 (man on phone); Total/CSTJF Pau France
p.5 (3D seismic evaluation); WesterGeco p.30 (GPS pipeline maintenance).

*Although every effort has been made to trace and contact copyright holders before
publication, this has not been possible in some cases. We apologize for any apparent
infringement of copyright and if notified, the publisher will be pleased to rectify any
errors or omissions at the earliest opportunity.*

*The author and publisher would like to thank the following people who assisted in the
development of this title:* Dr. Sulaiman Alruban, Caroline Brandt, Badria Dehrab,
Jon Dunn, Mohamed Omar Emhemmed, Sameera A. Al Gharabally, Peter
Hardcastle, Balia Jolamanova, Márcia Luíza F. Maciel E. Leão, Simon Macartney,
Elisabeth Michalkiewicz, M. Kamal Sawwan, Tahani Al-Shaher, Crispin Sharp,
Ekaterina Simakova, Eurof Thomas, Crispin Tucker, Svetlana E. Ustyuzhina.

Special thanks are also due to: Peter Astley, Anna Gunn, Roberta Calderbank,
Steve Innes, Eileen Flannigan (author: Grammar Reference), and Ben Francis
(author: Glossary, Website).